D0565420

WHAT WILL YOUR GRANDCHILDREN SEE WHEN THEY LOOK UP?

V 1.0

Authors:

Michael S. Yeo, Gary Gates, Amita Kashyap, Alexander G. Hunt,
Zohar Hoter, Mitchell F. Bernards, and Justin Inman

Edited by:

David G. Ullman

ISBN-13: 978-1539892106
ISBN-10: 1539892107

CONTENTS

INTRODUCTION:

WHY THIS BOOK EXISTS

Professor David G. Ullman

Why this book exists

This book explores the future of aviation. It was developed by students enrolled in a class titled "The History of Aviation 1800-2200" offered in 2016 through the Honors College at Oregon State University. The course reviewed the history of atmospheric flight and, in parallel worked with the students to generate a vision of the future, specifically at a time when their grandchildren become aware of objects in the sky - about 2050.

The course description used to tease students to take this two credit hour, ten week, colloquium style course was:

> *Machines that fly have evolved for over 200 years and the arc is continuing - beginning with George Cayley in the early 19th century, through the Wright Brothers in the early 20th century, the era of records in the 1920s and 30s, the evolution of the war machine in the 1940s, the pilotless eye in the sky of the last 10 years, and on to the promise of unmanned, composite, electric air taxis. This course examines the development of the technologies, politics and cultural attitudes toward commercial, military, general aviation and science fiction air travel. We examine the trajectory of these evolutions and try to predict what air travel will look like by mid 21st century. What will your grandchildren see when they look up, how will they fly?*

The course spent the first five weeks exploring the evolution of flight from its prehistory, the early hops by the Wright Brothers, to hypersonic jets. Parallel to this we explored the promise of things to come. This promise is centered on the evolution of new demands, methods of propulsion and materials as will be seen.

This book is structured around this introductory chapter written by the editor and professor for the course, followed by a series of student-written chapters on important considerations about the future of aviation. The book ends with a final chapter, written by the team, summarizing what their grandchildren will see when they look up. Of course, in the words of the Danish proverb; *"Det er vanskeligt at spaa, især naar det gælder Fremtiden"* or; "It is difficult to make predictions, especially about the future."

This introduction gives a brief overview of the chapters and their authors. In each chapter the author provides sufficient background to support their vision of the future and attempts to draw out the drivers that encourage development and the factors that will be used to measure progress. Drivers are what fuel change. In aviation the drivers are often war, the desire to set records, or commercial efforts to make money. Of course the chapter authors can not foresee future wars like WWI and WWII during which there was great advances in aviation technology. But, the recent advances in drones and air vehicle autonomy have been driven by smaller wars in the Mid-East.

The Chapters

As the text evolves, electric propulsion is seen a major technology in the future of aviation. Thus, the first chapter, written by Michael Yeo, a Junior in Electrical and Computer Engineering, focuses on battery and fuel cell evolution. Writing this chapter in 2016 is a big challenge as it is a time when electric cars are showing great promise and, at the same time, the price of a barrel of oil is depressed, slowing electric vehicle growth and adoption. In spite of this slow-down, there are large investments being made in battery technologies, design and manufacturing. Tesla's Gigafactory is just coming on line as this book is being written. Further, the level of research into electrical energy storage is at an all time high.

Michael also addresses the promise of fuel cells. Like batteries, 2016 has seen leaps in their promise and the potential for hydrogen fueled electric aircraft. Michael explores what it will take for these evolving technologies to have an effect in the air.

Another area where change is bound to occur is in the development and use of new materials. While composites have been used in general aviation airplanes since the 1970s, they have been slow to be adopted. Still, only a small percentage of general aviation airplanes are made of composites and it was only with the introduction of Boeing's 787 Dreamliner in 2011 and Airbuses latest aircraft that primarily composite airplanes entered commercial service. Thus, in this chapter, Gary Gates a Junior in Mechanical, Industrial, and Manufacturing Engineering explores not only how composites will influence future air travel, but how new materials and manufacturing methods will make airplanes less expensive to build and maintain.

As important as electrical power and new materials are to the future of aviation, autonomy is seen as a major change that will occur over the next 35 years. Amita Kashyap a Senior in Bioresource Research: Genomics/Bioinformatics grasps this future at a time when autonomous cars are rapidly evolving and there is active debate about their place in society. This is an especially difficult chapter as it was less than a month ago that the book's editor and Professor his first semi-autonomous car (a 2016 Tesla). It could maintain traffic spacing, change lanes and read the speed limit, all without his input. In 2016 this is a big deal, but the future ….

While electric airplanes may or may not make up a significant portion of what is in future skies, it is likely that other forms of propulsion will make up the fleet. In the fourth chapter Alex Hunt, a Freshman in Mechanical, Industrial, and Manufacturing Engineering explores what else, besides electricity, will power the airplanes of the future. Things change very slowly in the aircraft industry so; there is a good chance that fossil fuels will still be in the mix. The question is how to make the use of fossil fuels more efficiently and what other forms of propulsion might take a market share.

Where the first four chapters focused on specific technologies, the next three address specific types of aircraft, beginning with airliners. Zohar Hoter, a Sophomore in Mechanical, Industrial, and Manufacturing Engineering, begins his look into the future by describing how current passenger travel is safe and relatively affordable. Yet it is very noisy near airports, inconvenient and very non-sustainable. At the same time, it has shrunk the world and the airline business continues to grow. Zohar explores how commercial air travel will become more efficient and faster over the next thirty five years.

2016 is also a time of great change in the public's awareness of drones. Where the military has made use of them for last ten years they have exploded on the national scene. In chapter six Mitch Bernards, a Junior in Mechanical, Industrial and Manufacturing Engineering develops the different types of drones currently in use and how they may evolve in the future. At the current time, drone evolution is very dependent on battery development. For example, currently, quad-copter drones, no matter how large are limited to 15 minutes of flight time due to battery energy density limitations.

After WWII there was a big effort to put an airplane in every-man's garage. Evidence of this can be seen at any small airport where private pilots fly many airplanes designed and manufactured during that period - Aeroncas, Stintsons, Pipers, Ercoupes…. In chapter seven Justin Inman, a Senior in Mechanical, Industrial and Manufacturing Engineering brings this concept up-to-date exploring how Personal Air Vehicles (PAVs) or "air taxis" might evolve over the next thirty five years. The PAV vision is to develop air vehicles for personal travel that are safe, quiet, on-demand, sustainable, fast (door-to-door), and publicly acceptable; all factors currently not met by general aviation

Finally, in chapter eight, the findings of the class are summarized in an effort to answer the question that is the title of this book: *What Will Your Grandchildren See When They Look Up?* This chapter itemizes ten predictions developed by the authors and supported in their individual chapters.

Note that this book has been given designation "V 1.0" to indicate that it will be updated in subsequent classes. Beyond updating the material, subsequent versions will add new material based on the predictions and other material in Chapter 8. Realize that the material in this book is almost instantly out of date. For example, while going to press announcements were made about the first human carrying hydrogen fuel cell aircraft fight and an Amazon autonomous drone's first delivery of a parcel to a customer. These types of announcements, which mostly support the predictions, are currently an almost daily occurrence.

For how we wrote and published this book in ten weeks, or the experience of managing a team of students writing a book, see www.davidullman.com/aeronautics/WWGS-notes.pdf.

CHAPTER 1:

WILL ELECTRIC AIRCRAFT TAKE CHARGE OF THE AIRWAYS?

THE FUTURE OF ELECTRIC AIRPLANES

Michael S. Yeo, Junior

Electrical and Computer Engineering

Introduction

Between the electric "hoverboards" that catch on fire, the electric Shinkansen bullet trains in Japan, and the 1.15 million electric cars in use today, transportation has never been more electrically driven. However, while land and sea-based electric vehicles exhibit great promise in their niche markets, electric aircraft are still slow to take-off. Battery limitations (ex. mass and volume vs. output), strict FAA regulations, and commercial scalability are just some of the challenges that make "electric airplanes a far steeper challenge than electric cars"[i]. Still, electric aircraft have undeniably improved over time and research by Boeing, Airbus, NASA, and others in this field is at an all-time high[ii]. So when, if ever, will electric aircraft take charge of the airways?

It Started as a Bold Prediction:
History of Electric Aircraft

On October 8, 1883, in the quiet suburbs of Auteuil, France, crowds were gathering to see the Tissandier brothers fly the world's first airship powered by an electric motor[iii]. The 92-foot long airship struggled off the ground as the 500-pound engine and battery pack pushed the dirigible to its weight limits[iv]. Once airborne, the measly 1.5 hp engine propelled the airship at just 3 mph in calm winds. Plus, the battery drained so quickly that the airship was unable to complete a single 360° turn. In fact, according to historian C.B. Hayward, the airship had several "inherent limitations" such that "no one familiar with the drawbacks" would fly the "freak". Yet, at the end of their flight, the Tissandier brothers not only proved electric-powered flight to be possible, but they made two bold predictions about the future of electric-driven aviation[v]:

1. Electric-powered air vehicles will "improve exponentially over the next century."
2. Electric-powered air vehicles will "dominate the skies."

Almost immediately, these predictions seemed prophetic when Charles Renard and Arthur Krebs improved upon the Tissandier airship to create *La France* the following year. Armed with an 8 hp engine and a larger battery, *La France* traveled 8 km (5 mi.) in 23 minutes to not only be the first fully controlled free-flight of an air vehicle, but the first round-trip flight as well. However, *La France* also revealed three major flaws with electric-powered flight at that time:

1. Batteries had very bad storage/weight ratios (heavy), severely limiting speed and range.
2. Batteries were one-use only (non-rechargeable) and depleted quickly; very costly.
3. Electric motors were susceptible to burning out, reducing the reliability of the airship.

These shortcomings contributed to a transitional period in the early 1900s, where developments in the traditional airplane (i.e. Wright brothers, Santos-Dumont, etc.) and improvements in the internal combustion engine placed electric aircraft development on a long-term hiatus. Even when electric motors became powerful enough, light enough, and reliable enough to power a full-sized aircraft by the 1950s, little headway was made in developing electric aircraft. Not even the inception of the lead-acid battery, the first rechargeable battery, could turn the tides. In fact, it took until 1973 (89 years) for a full-sized electric airplane to be successful.

The reason for this delay stemmed directly from the horrendously low power-to-weight ratios of batteries from that era. The sheer weight of the batteries required for flight even made building small models challenging, let alone the full-scale implementation. As a result, individuals who attempted to build an electric aircraft during the early-to-mid 20th century found that either the plane was too heavy to get airborne or the batteries did not provide enough power for sustained flight. It wasn't until the early 1970s, when nickel-cadmium (NiCad) batteries were well-developed, that electric airplane development started to ramp up again. After that, the innovation "floodgates" opened.

Following the NiCad battery, which had a far superior power-to-weight ratio from older batteries, solar cells, hydrogen fuel cells, and improved battery (ex. alkaline, lithium-ion, etc.) technologies were quickly developed in the late 20th century. In conjunction with the ever-improving electric motor, these developments helped drive electric aircraft success. Table 1 displays some key examples in how electric aircraft have developed over the past 133 years. As you can see, many of the innovations and all-time firsts in electric aviation took place within the past 43 years (1973 to present). And there seems to be no signs of it slowing anytime soon.

In fact, just six weeks prior to writing this chapter, two new electric aircraft were tested. First, the Robinson R44 electric helicopter completed its maiden flight - the first-ever manned, battery-powered helicopter. The R44 was capable of flying for 20 minutes and reaching speeds upwards of 92 mph over its 34-mile journey. Researchers ultimately hope that, one day, the R44 can serve as an EPSAROD vehicle (Electrically Powered Semi-Autonomous Rotorcraft for

Organ Delivery) to efficiently deliver transplantable organs to major hospitals under a clean carbon footprint[vi]. The second aircraft is the German HY4 - the first hydrogen fuel cell-powered four-seater passenger airplane. The HY4 flew for 18 minutes and capped out at 124 mph. Unlike the R44, the international team that built the HY4 are reaching for the stars in their pursuit of reforming passenger flights around the world to be emission-free[vii].

Model	Year	Details	Source
Renaud and Kreb's La France	1884	• First fully controllable airship and free-flight. • First full round-trip flight (land back at start). • 960 lbs. battery and 8 hp, 350 lbs. motor. • Traveled 8 km in 23 minutes per trip.	Winter 1933, 49-50[viii]
PKZ-1	1917	• Designed to replace hydrogen observation balloons in use during WWI. • Tethered to an electric power source on the ground; not able to fly freely. • Flew vertically up to a height of 15 meters. • 190 hp, 420 lbs. motor and no battery. • Motor burned out on fourth test flight due to excess strain from lifting three passengers. • Only one full-scale version was produced.	Petroczy 2008[ix]
Militky MB-E1	1973	• First full-sized, manned aircraft to fly under its own electrical power; no external source. • Per flight maximum: 12 minutes at 112 mph and at an altitude of 380 meters. • 350 lbs. battery and 13 hp, 30 lbs. motor.	Taylor 1974, 573[x]
Alisport Silent Club	1997	• First commercially available production electric aircraft (single-seater sailplane). • Per flight maximum: 13 minutes at 112 mph and at an altitude of 700 meters. • 88 lbs. battery and 17 hp, 19 lbs. motor.	Silent 2002[xi]
Electravia BL1E Electra	2007	• First aircraft powered by an electric motor and batteries to be registered with an airworthiness certificate. • Per flight maximum: 48 minutes for 50 km at 60 mph. • 104 lbs. battery and 24 hp, 27 lbs. motor.	Bremner 2008[xii]
Boeing EC-003 FCD	2009	• First full-sized, manned aircraft powered solely by hydrogen fuel cells. • Per flight maximum: 20 minutes at 60 mph and at an altitude of 1,000 meters.	Koehler 2008, 44-45[xiii]
Chip Yates' Rutan Long-EZ	2009	• Set 5 new aviation world records in 4 weeks under the 100% electric aircraft category. • Per flight maximum: 15 km distance at 202.6 mph and at an altitude of 4800 meters. • 525 lbs. battery and 258 hp, 120 lbs. motor. • Experienced many in-flight electrical issues.	Paur 2013[xiv]
Pipistrel Taurus G4	2011	• First place winner of NASA's 2011 Green Flight Challenge - a competition striving to make passenger aircraft more efficient. • First four-seat aircraft to fly with just electric power. • 531 lbs. battery and 195 hp, 121 lbs. motor. • Per flight maximum: > 322 km distance at 113.6 mph. • 403.5 PMPGe (passenger miles per gallon equivalent). In comparison, the G36 Bonanza, a popular general aviation aircraft, gets 104.98 PMPG on gasoline.	Harbaugh 2016[xv] and Wells 2011[xvi]

Table 1: Examples showing how electric aircraft have evolved throughout history.

While it is undeniable that electric-powered aircraft have "improved exponentially" from its roots, we have yet to see them in mass overhead; electric aircraft are not even close to "dominat[ing] the skies" as the Tissandier brothers have predicted. So what is keeping electric aircraft parked on the runways? Is it due to the current limitations of electric motors (ex. the Chip Yates' Rutan Long-EZ)? Could it stem from the strict FAA regulations regarding electric aircraft use (including drones and PAVs)? Or maybe it's due to the recent depression in oil and jet fuel (AV Gas) prices? The correct answer is all of the above. Each of these issues or points have contributed in slowing electric aircraft development. However, at the very forefront, "the biggest hurdle for [electric-powered aviation] is battery technology, particularly the battery's specific energy, or the amount of energy it can store for a given amount of weight" [i].

Indeed, the same issue that hampered the Tissandier airship, *La France*, and the aforementioned 89-year lapse in advancement, is the primary reason why we don't see more electric aircraft flying today. Simply put, batteries store too little energy and weigh too much. As a result, modern electric aircraft are severely limited in how fast, how far, and how long they can travel. Their performance pales in comparison to the gasoline-powered aircraft we see today.

This fact is evident in Table 2, where the flight capabilities and "fuel" weights of the electrically-powered R44 helicopter and HY4 airplane are directly compared to their gasoline counterparts - the R44 Raven II and the Cessna 172R, respectively. As you can see, the electric R44 is not only significantly slower, but it is only capable of flying for a tenth of the distance and duration as the gasoline R44. And while this distinction is not immediately noticeable between the HY4 and the Cessna 172R, there are two things to note. First, the HY4's flight duration and distance values are calculated theoretical maximums, where the plane's speed, altitude, and carrying load are optimized. As such, the actual values are most likely on the lower end of the range, if they are on the range at all. Second, the likewise values for the Cessna 172R were measured under controlled conditions, where the plane had a maximum payload, as well as 45 minutes of fuel still remaining. Hence, these actual values are most likely higher. When we consider these two things, we can see that the electric HY4 underperforms the Cessna 172R (slower with half the distance and duration).

The primary cause for this disparity is tied to the "fuel" weight seen in Table 2. For instance, the batteries on the electric R44 weigh three times more than a full tank of fuel on the Raven II. The same can be said between the HY4 and the Cessna 172R. When we attempt to scale this up to a commercial airliner like the popular Boeing 747-400, not only will the electric version underperform the gasoline model, but the actual "fuel" system would weigh over a million pounds. With this much weight, the plane wouldn't be able to move that well, let alone fly.

Model	Max. Flight Duration	Max. Flight Distance	Max. Flight Speed	Fuel / Power Source Weight	Source
Robinson R44 (battery-powered)	20 minutes	34 miles	92 mph	~ 1,100 lbs. (batteries only)	Clarke 2016[vi]
Robinson R44 Raven II	196 minutes	350 miles	150 mph	301 lbs. (full tank load)	Robinson 2005[xvii]

German HY4 (fuel-cell powered)	235 - 323 minutes*	466 - 932 miles*	124 mph	~ 930 lbs. (fuel cell, battery, and storage)	Kallo 2015[xviii]
Cessna 172R	396 minutes**	801 miles**	142 mph	337 lbs. (full tank load)	Palt 2016[xix]
Boeing 747-400	948 minutes***	8,383 miles***	624 mph	344,283 lbs. (full tank load)	The 2010[xx]

* = theoretical maximums based on based on optimized speed, altitude, and loads
** = flying 12,000 ft. high at 55% power with maximum payload and 45 minutes of reserve fuel remaining
*** = full passenger payload

Table 2: Flight performance comparison between modern electric and gasoline-powered aircraft.

Ultimately, this poses the question, "Where is the future of electric aircraft headed towards?"

And it Continues as a Bold Prediction: Projecting Ahead

To address this question, this chapter will attempt to project whether or not electric aircraft will take charge of the airways (i.e. more than 50% of airborne aircraft are purely electric) by the year 2050. In order to arrive at a conclusion, a couple different topics will be explored.

Since the main component holding back electric aircraft is the limitations of energy storage devices, or accumulators, this chapter will heavily explore the two main types used in today's aviation world - batteries and hydrogen fuel cells. By looking at the historical progression and current capabilities (and limitations) of both of these technologies, this chapter will attempt to project where batteries and fuel cells will be by 2050 (and what that means for electric aircraft).

In addition, this chapter will consider two major drivers concurrently present for electric aircraft development - environmental concerns and drone development - and see how each driver might impact future development in this field.

Finally, these points will be combined to update the Tissandier brothers' 1883 prediction and arrive at an academic consensus for the state of electric aircraft in the year 2050.

Battery Technology

Batteries are, by far, the most common type of energy storage device in use today. From classic alkaline AA batteries, to the traditional lead-acid car batteries, to even the lithium polymer batteries running our mobile phones, batteries are prevalent nearly everywhere we look. However, before we delve into the guts of battery technology, we need to know what a battery is.

By definition, a "battery" is "a container consisting of one or more cells, in which chemical energy is converted into electricity and used as a power source"[xxi]. With this in mind, let us proceed.

Brief History of the Battery

Alessandro Volta, an Italian physicist, is credited for inventing the voltaic pile - the first true electric battery - in 1799. Created by crudely stacking copper and zinc discs that were separated by brine-soaked cardboard, the voltaic pile produced a stable current and provided constant charge to its load. However, due to its design, the voltaic pile, at best, exhibited a maximum battery life of only 60 minutes at an abysmal 10% efficiency rating[xxii].

Over the next 60 years, scientists focused on improving the voltaic pile. As seen in Table 3, each new battery was a direct improvement over its predecessor. These batteries became the first practical sources of electricity. Particularly, the Daniell Cell was not only an industry standard for powering telegraph networks, but it was also the historical basis for the contemporary definition of the volt as a unit[xxiii].

Battery Name	Year	Inventor	Battery Based On (Predecessor)	Improvement on Predecessor
Daniell Cell	1836	John Frederic Daniell	Voltaic Pile	Used copper sulfate and an earthenware container; improved battery life and current flow.
Bird's Cell	1837	Golding Bird	Daniell Cell	Replaced cardboard separators with plaster; improved reliability.
Grove Cell	1839	William Robert Grove	Bird's Cell	Replaced zinc cathode with platinum; improved current and doubled the voltage.
Grenet Cell	1859	Eugene Grenet	Grenet Cell	Used dilute sulphuric acid and eliminated the earthenware container; improved voltage.

Table 3: Examples of the first practical batteries.

However, each battery was one-use only; once the chemical reaction was spent, the battery was permanently drained. That is, until Gaston Planté invented the lead-acid battery in 1859 - the first-ever battery that could be recharged via a reverse passing current. Consisting of two lead sheets separated by spiral rubber strips, Planté's battery used sulphuric acid in conjunction with a wire and a lead dioxide to produce a current[xxiv]. This basic design and principal has not changed much since 1859. The lead-acid battery marks the first battery that is still commonly in use during this chapter's authorship (car batteries). Interestingly, each major battery that was invented after 1859 shared two commonalities with the lead-acid battery:

1. Rechargeability
2. Heavy mass relative to the energy capacity

Over the next 157 years, many types of batteries were created, including, but not limited to: the zinc-carbon cell, nickel-cadmium, alkaline, nickel metal-hydride, and lithium-ion. Each of these batteries improved upon the efficiency and energy capacity of the lead-acid battery.

Current Capabilities and Limitations

Currently, there are several types of batteries in commercial use. Table 4 displays the four main types of batteries utilized today (lead-acid, nickel-cadmium, nickel metal-hydride, and lithium-ion/polymer), including Tesla batteries (electric cars). The theoretical max values for lithium-composite and lithium-air batteries are included as well. For the purposes of analyzing electric airplanes, these values are contrasted with the current aviation gasoline (AV Gas) values.

Battery Type	Avg. Cost $/kWh	Wh/L	Wh/kg	Wh/kg Deliverable
Lead-Acid	$100 − $200	60 − 110	30 − 50	23 − 38
NiCad	$1,000 − $1,500	50 − 150	40 − 60	32 − 40
NiMH	$450 − $700	140 − 300	50 − 60	40 − 48
Lithium-Ion Incl. Polymer	$250 − $500	250 − 670	100 − 265	90 − 239
Tesla	$150 − $500	700	195	172
Li-X Max*	-------------------	∼ 2,850	∼ 5,200	∼ 5,148
Lithium-Air*	-------------------	∼ 6,200	∼ 12,000	∼ 10,200
AV Gas	$140	10,000	13,500	4,200

Table 4: Statistics of batteries currently in use today (* denotes future projections and theoretical values) in comparison with AV Gas[xxv]. Source verified through secondary sources.

To fully understand what each value in Table 4 represents, consider the following definitions:

- Avg. Cost $/kWh: Average **cost** in dollars for the unit to generate one kilowatt-hour.
- Wh/L: Volumetric energy density, or the number of watt-hours that can be stored in the unit per liter of physical space; determines the **volume** of the unit.
- Wh/kg: Gravimetric energy density, or the number of watt-hours that can be stored in the unit per kilogram of mass; determines the **mass** of the unit (assuming 100% efficiency).
- Wh/kg Deliverable: Same as Wh/kg, but factors in the efficiency of the unit, as well as the downstream components, including the wiring, connections, engines, etc.

By knowing what each column in Table 4 means, we can see how modern batteries compare to AV Gas. In general, while electric engines are far more efficient than IC engines (90% to 25%), batteries require substantially more space and weight than AV Gas to match the latter's energy production. For example, let's consider the upper-end of lithium-ion batteries currently on the market today. At 670 Wh/L and 239 Wh/kg deliverable, this Li-ion battery will take up to nearly 15 times the physical space and weigh almost 17 times more than the energy-equivalent in AV Gas. Plus, this isn't even factoring in the battery's casing, wires, or the need to manage its heat protection. When we then consider an airplane's physical constraints and the energy required to get airborne, we quickly realize the main issue with purely using batteries for flight.

Table 5 accentuates this point. The estimated energy specifications (i.e. max fuel capacity, takeoff speed and power, engine thrust, average load, and the amount energy consumed when cruising) of three popular and widely-used commercial airliners are noted. By comparing these values with the specs of a Boeing 787 Li-ion battery, the following was found:

- Number of Boeing 787 batteries required to power the engines to reach takeoff speed (V2), assuming it takes a minute to do so.
- Number of Boeing 787 batteries that the fuel tanks could volumetrically hold if we swapped the AV Gas with batteries.
- Number of batteries required to cover the energy expenditure per hour of normal flight at cruising altitude and speed, assuming no turbulence or abnormality.
- Amount of energy in megajoules that the IC engines could output by burning a full tank of AV Gas.
- Amount of energy in megajoules that an average electric engine could output by consuming the charge of a "tank full" (see second point above) of Boeing 787 batteries.

Boeing 787 Battery (Li-Ion)					
Model	# of Batteries Needed for Takeoff	# of Batteries Needed to Fill Fuel Capacity	# of Batteries Needed to Cover In-Flight Consumption per Hour	Energy Stored as Fuel (MJ)	Energy Stored as Batteries (MJ)
Boeing 747-8F	3.0 million	6,600	28,000	8.5 mil	41,000
Boeing 747-8I	3.0 million	6,900	28,000	8.9 mil	43,000
Airbus A320	5.6 million	870	5,200	1.1 mil	5,400

Table 5: 787 Dreamliner lithium-ion battery capabilities vs. commercial airplanes[xxvi].

By looking at these calculated values, we come to the following general conclusions about battery-powered commercial passenger airliners:

- Mass Comparison
  - The amount of batteries required to successfully takeoff is about 452 to 644

times heavier than the amount of AV Gas needed.

- The amount of batteries required to cover per-hour in-flight energy consumption is about 3 to 5 times heavier than the amount of AV Gas needed.
- Each Boeing 787 Dreamliner battery roughly weighs 28 kg (62 lbs.). Therefore, the minimum battery load to successfully fly a commercial aircraft (Boeing 747 in this case) for one hour is approximately 84 gigagrams, or 84 million kg. Note that the maximum AV Gas fuel capacity for a Boeing 747 is only 183,380 kg.
- Volume Comparison
  - Using the values from the mass comparison, the minimum battery volume needed to fly a Boeing 747 for one hour is about 84 megalitres, or 84 million litres. Note that the maximum AV Gas fuel capacity for a Boeing 747 is only 183,380 litres.
- Energy Density Comparison
  - The energy density of AV Gas is 162 times greater than the 787 Li-ion battery.

As you can see, the limited energy density and weight of today's batteries are inadequate to use as an airplane's only source of energy. Even when we scale down and look at an electric drone, the principles hold firm. For instance, most high-end, commercially available quadcopters (size being less than a cubic yard) take several hours to fully charge and only run for a few minutes. This is due to scalability. As the size of the aircraft changes, other parametrics like weight limit, available space, and power consumption follows. For example, a Boeing 787 has more available space and can take on more weight than a Cessna 172, but it requires far more power to operate. The ratio between space/weight vs. power is relatively proportional, which explains why both a quadcopter and the R44 helicopter run for less than 30 minutes on a given charge; similar times.

Beyond the energy density issue, each type of battery has its own unique shortcomings. For instance, not only are lead-acid batteries at risk for chemical corrosion and acid leakage, but they pose environmental concerns during disposal. In terms of electric aircraft, Li-ion and Li-ion polymer batteries are most commonly utilized (used by the R44, Rutan Long-EZ, and the BL1E) due to their high energy density. However, Li-ion batteries also have strict charging cycles that require monitored "feeding" and "draining" of the battery. As seen by Figure 1, not only do specific voltage and current values determine when a charging cycle starts (precondition or minimum) or stops (termination), but the charging rate is also specified (slope). Even charging slightly too early, too late, too little, or too much can lead to degradation of the battery's capacity and/or runtime. However, the main concern of Li-ion batteries is overheating and ignition.

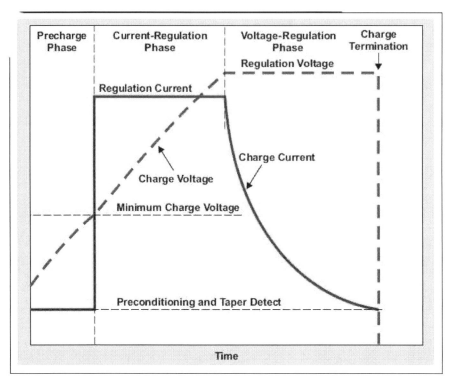

Figure 1: Lithium-ion battery recommended charging cycle[xxvii].

Li-ion batteries have been known to quickly overheat due to poor maintenance or improper ventilation/cooling/charging, which sometimes leads to fires. The fires are not only self-sustained by the battery itself, but they have to be extinguished with a Halon-based agent (non-liquid). And when these fires start inside of an airplane in-flight, catastrophe is almost guaranteed. Most recently, in 2013, Boeing's entire fleet of 787 Dreamliners were grounded for over six months by the FAA due to spontaneous smoke and fires breaking out of the lithium-ion battery packs. Interestingly, an in-depth investigation led by Boeing found no single cause for these thermal events. The only way that Boeing could solve the issue was to spend millions of dollars to retrofit the entire fleet of 787s with fire-proof battery cases, thermally-triggered ventilation systems, and other safeguards[xxviii]. Following these events, the FAA placed strict regulations on Li-ion batteries; Li-ion-wise, cargo on passenger planes were banned and luggage had stringent size and quantity limits[xxix].

Overall, regardless of safety or energy density issues, we can see that, as of now, modern batteries are not suitable for solely powering electric aircraft, especially on major airliners.

Future Outlook

While batteries may not suffice now, will they be able to meet the demands of electric aircraft by 2050? To answer this question, let's look at the progression of the Li-ion battery - the most widely-used and energy-packed battery in the aviation market today. The graph in Figure 2 plots the historical Wh/kg, Wh/L, price/Wh, and Wh/kg deliverable of an average Li-ion battery from 1991 (first commercialization) to 2005, as well as 2016. In addition, two trend lines are added to the Wh/kg deliverable plot (i.e. energy density) in order to create a "cone of uncertainty" (best-case and worst-case) projection of Li-ion in 2050. The black (top) trend line represents a best-case exponential growth curve that is based on the most optimistic projections (for 2025) made by experts in the battery industry. The red (bottom) trend line represents a worst-case linear improvement of the Li-ion's energy density. A linear trend line was used since we can arguably assume that the capabilities of electric motors and Li-ion batteries, which are both relatively newer technologies, will not flatten out or digress in the coming years. Thus, by 2050, Li-ion batteries have a projected energy density of approximately 500 - 1,950 Wh/kg deliverable.

To interpret this range, we need to harken back to two values seen in Table 4. First, AV Gas currently has an energy density of 4,200 Wh/kg deliverable. This value will likely continue to improve, albeit slowly, as IC engines become more efficient. Second, the theoretical maximum energy density for all Lithium composites is 5,148 Wh/kg deliverable. Hence, Li-ion has the potential to surpass the energy output of AV Gas in the future, but not by 2050. Even under the best-case scenario, Li-ion batteries are less than half as energy-packed as AV Gas by 2050, at 1,950 Wh/kg deliverable to 4,200 Wh/kg deliverable.

Still, at 1,950 Wh/kg deliverable (or eight times the average of today's Li-ion battery), electric-powered aircraft like the Taurus G4 and BL1E Electra (see Table 1) will be capable of flying for several hours at a time. And while this level of performance might not match that of a gasoline-powered aircraft like the Cessna 172R, it is definitely viable as a successful general aviation aircraft. Even when we consider the worst-case scenario of 500 Wh/kg deliverable (or twice the average of today's Li-ion battery), electric-powered aircraft will be able to fly for more than one hour. This dramatically increases the range that these aircraft can travel, opening possibilities for commercial and non-commercial use, including flying clubs and flight training.

However, while this level of power might suffice for drones and light aircraft, it still falls short of the energy output required by commercial airliners. Furthermore, even if the energy density of Li-ion rises, the physical shortcomings of the Li-ion battery will likely remain, even if to a lesser degree. This includes the degradation, overheating, and safety issues discussed earlier. And this will continue to pose a threat to all aircraft, particularly to major airliners.

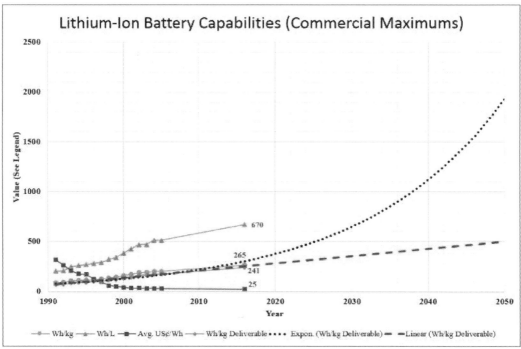

Figure 2: Lithium-ion battery statistics from 1991 to 2016, including two trend lines: (1) best-case exponential growth curve and (2) worst-case linear growth curve[xxx].

Looking beyond lithium-ion, there are currently several new battery technologies being developed and tested in laboratories and universities around the world. These include gold nanowire batteries, magnesium batteries, solid-state batteries, and graphene batteries. Of these, the most promising is the lithium-air battery (Li-Air), which uses lithium oxidation to induce a current flow. As seen in Table 4, the theoretical maximum energy density almost triples that of AV Gas. However, like most of the other new battery technologies, Li-air batteries are still several years away from being fully developed, let alone commercialized. Particularly, challenges in recharging, stability, and spontaneous discharging outline just some of the issues facing Li-air batteries. Still, with battery research and funding at an all-time high (and growing) and new discoveries being made on the daily, it is possible for Li-ion to be usurped by 2050.

Fuel Cell Technology

While lesser known, fuel cells are the second-most common type of electric storage device in use today. With applications ranging from powering NASA's satellites and space capsules, to providing backup power for industrial and residential buildings, to even running fuel cell vehicles (ex. cars, buses, boats, lifts, etc.), fuel cells play an important role in today's society. While batteries and fuel cells may seem similar, there is one stark difference between them.

By definition, a "fuel cell" is a "device that converts the chemical energy from a fuel into electricity through a chemical reaction with an oxidizing agent"[xxxi]. Generally, modern fuel cells generate energy by reacting stored hydrogen with oxygen, so they are often referred to as hydrogen fuel cells. While a battery produces energy from a chemical reaction stored inside of the battery itself, a fuel cell makes energy by reacting an oxidizer with fuel from an external source. However, both batteries and fuel cells use chemical processes.

Brief History of the Fuel Cell

While it is true that major fuel cell development didn't occur until the 1960s, the first fuel cell was actually invented in 1838. Indeed, a Welsh judge named William Robert Grove used iron sheets, copper, porcelain plates, dilute acid, and sulphate to invent the Grove voltaic cell - the world's first fuel cell. Beyond generating an intermittent current, the Grove voltaic cell had no practical use as an energy source[xxxii].

It would take over 100 years for the next major advancement to occur. However, progress ramped up tremendously. In 1939, Francis Thomas Bacon developed a 5 kW fuel cell using potassium hydroxide and nickel reactants. In the 1950s, hydrogen and oxygen were widely used as the reactants for fuel cells. During this time, General Electric teamed up with NASA and McDonnell Aircraft in Project Gemini, or NASA's second human spaceflight program. Here, fuel cells were used to power various systems on the rockets and spacecraft, leading to the first commercial use of fuel cells in 1959.

Over the next 57 years, many types of fuel cells were developed. These include, but are not limited to: Proton Exchange Membrane fuel cells (PEMFCs), phosphoric acid fuel cells (PAFCs), solid acid fuel cells (SAFCs), and alkaline fuel cells (AFCs).

Current Capabilities and Limitations

There are several types of fuel cells on the market today. In fact, the number of currently active fuel-cell variants outnumber the battery variants. However, for the purposes of this chapter, we will focus on the most-widely used fuel cell for electric airplanes - the Proton Exchange Membrane fuel cell (PEMFC); it was used on the HY4 and EC-003 FCD (see Table 1).

The graph in Figure 3 shows the average energy densities (in Wh/L) of PEMFC fuel cells under two different hydrogen pressure loads (5,000 and 10,000 psi), as well as the current energy densities of lead-acid (Pb-A), nickel metal-hydride (NiMH), lithium-ion (Li-ion), and U.S. Advanced Battery Consortium (USABC) batteries. As you can see, PEMFC fuel cells have nearly a 1.5-to-2 times greater energy density ratio than Li-ion batteries. Unfortunately, while this may seem significant, the difference between the two technologies still pales in comparison to the nearly thirty times greater 10,000 Wh/L energy density of AV Gas.

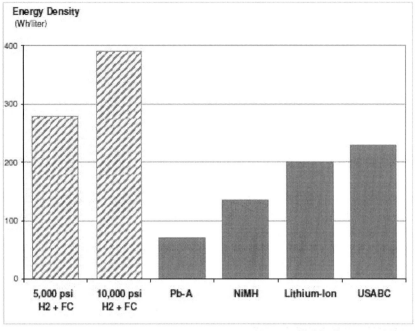

Figure 3: The energy density of PEMFC fuel cells under different hydrogen pressures vs. the energy density of various batteries[xxxiii].

In addition, like Li-ion batteries, PEMFC fuel cells have several shortcomings as well. These primarily include the following:

- Due to its design, the PEMFC fuel cell requires water to evaporate at exactly the same rate as it is introduced. This requires a high level of maintenance and precise water and air management. Otherwise, the fuel cell will become damaged and spontaneously fail.
- Produces high amounts of heat, so the temperature needs to be constantly regulated.
- Very high cost compared to Li-ion batteries (est. $67 per kW of power).
- In the United States, hydrogen production is relatively low. Also, a lack of an existing coast-to-coast hydrogen distribution infrastructure promotes high costs and low supply.
- Storage of pressurized hydrogen is a safety concern on aircraft, especially that of fire.

When we consider all of these parameters, we can see that modern fuel cells, likewise to Li-ion batteries, are not up to the task of running electric aircraft on their own.

Future Outlook

Unlike battery technology, the future of hydrogen fuel cells are less predictable. Due to the relatively recent commercialization of fuel cell technology, a lack of reliable empirical data makes it nearly impossible to project where fuel cells will stand by 2050 (i.e. the projection graph created for Li-ion batteries is not possible). Moreover, scientists cannot arrive at a theoretical maximum energy density value for any type of hydrogen fuel cell. Hence, their potential is completely unknown.

The only fact we can say for certain is that fuel cells are improving over time. Currently, the National Fuel Cell Research Center (NFCRC), the National Renewable Energy Laboratory (NREL), and many of the top engineering universities in the U.S. are working together to improve the efficiency and energy density of concurrently existing fuel cells. With millions of dollars of funding going into fuel cell research, including $35 million in 2015 alone, there is no doubt that constant progress can be made over the coming years.

Much like the Li-ion battery, it seems very unlikely that the energy density of fuel cells will reach anywhere near that of AV Gas by 2050. Thus, airliner applications seem out of the realm of possibility. However, likewise to the worst-case scenario explored for Li-ion batteries, even a small improvement to PEMFC fuel cells (say a factor of two) will allow fuel cell-powered aircraft to be a viable alternative in general aviation. This is exemplified by the current flight capabilities of the HY4 in Table 2. Even though the HY4 underperforms the Cessna 172R, the plane is still able to fly for a couple of hours at a good speed. As fuel cell technology improves, planes like the HY4 could easily fly for several hours and perhaps approach the capabilities of gasoline-powered aircraft like the Cessna 172R. The potential is definitely there.

Societal Response

While we can see that battery and fuel cell technologies will undoubtedly evolve in the future, we have yet to explore why electric aircraft should follow suit. In order to explain this, we have to look at the main social drivers that are pushing for progress in electric aviation. Specifically, there are two major drivers that are currently in place for electric aircraft development: (1) environmental concerns and (2) drone advancement. Let's delve into each driver a bit deeper.

Driver: Environmental Concerns

Initially started in the 1970s, the environmentalist movement, or Green Movement, has ramped up in recent years due to both a political and social shift towards global warming awareness. In just the past 10 years, "clean" electric and hybrid vehicle sales have been at an all-time high. Also, the number of people biking to work (rather than driving) has increased by about 60% within the past decade[xxxiv]. Undoubtedly, emission awareness has never been higher.

The mode of transportation that produces the greatest amount of emissions and greenhouse gasses per trip (non-collectively) is the gasoline-powered airplane, as seen in Figure 4. Airplane travel alone accounts for about 3.4% of all global carbon emissions. Hence, there is a logical reason why individuals might push towards zero-emission electric airplanes, or at the very least, hybrid airplanes.

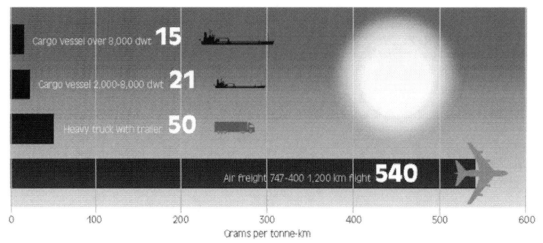

Figure 4: Emission comparison between different modes of transportation[xxxv].

Driver: Drone Advancement

Over the past decade, research into drone development has been at an all-time high. Regardless of whether we are talking about military drones for surveillance or quadcopters for recreational use, you will undoubtedly run into a recent news article outlining the newest developments in this field. However, the one key detail about drones is that they are usually electrically-powered, not gasoline-powered. This is due to the relatively small size of the drones, their short-travel radii, and the fact that electric motors are easy to control for movement and stability. As a direct consequence, the interest in improving electric aircraft will directly correlate from the interest in improving drone technology. As one progresses, the other will invariably follow.

Conclusion

Electric aircraft have definitely come a long way since the Tissandier brothers made their maiden flight in 1883. Interestingly, when we look back on the Tissandier brothers' optimism from 133 years ago, it is astonishing to see how close, yet so far, their visions were from reality. Electric aircraft did improve exponentially, albeit over the course of more than a century. However, the limitations in energy storage density prevented aircraft from "dominating the skies" then and now. Yet, as modern aircraft like the Taurus G4, R44, and HY4 expand the limits of electric-powered aviation closer to practical use, such a future seems to be on the near horizon.

The key for electric aviation is improving the energy densities of accumulators. By looking at the current capabilities and limitations of Li-ion batteries and PEMFC fuel cells, we found neither technology to be suitable for purely powering electric aircraft as of now. However, with research, funding, and interest at an ever-increasing peak, these energy storage devices will undoubtedly improve in the coming years. And while the magnitude of this advancement is unknown, and most likely inadequate for airliner applications, even the most minor increase in energy density will allow electric aircraft to be viable in general aviation. In addition, growing environmental concerns and advancements in drones are pushing electric aviation forward.

Overall, while it is uncertain if electric aircraft will dominate the airways by 2050, we can confidently make the following prediction:

> *We will see more electric-powered general aviation aircraft overhead,*
> *including small passenger aircraft like the HY4, as well as drones.*

[i] Masunaga, Samantha. "No Flying Tesla?" Los Angeles Times, September 9, 2016. Accessed December 2, 2016. http://www.latimes.com/business/la-fi-electric-aircraft-20160830-snap-story.html.

[ii] "Research Funding in 2016/17: A Global Overview." Laserglow Technologies. March 27, 2016. Accessed December 02, 2016. https://www.laserglow.com/page/news-apr16.

[iii] Swopes, Bryan R. "Tissandier Electric Airship." This Day in Aviation. October 8, 2016. Accessed November 25, 2016. https://www.thisdayinaviation.com/tag/tissandier-electric-airship/.

[iv] Hayward, Charles B. Types of Aeroplanes. Chicago, IL: American School of Correspondence, 1912, Pg 160-161.

[v] Ibid pg163

[vi] Clarke, Chris. "The First Electric Helicopter Will Carry Body Parts." Popular Mechanics. November 04, 2016. Accessed December 03, 2016. http://www.popularmechanics.com/flight/a23696/first-manned-electric-helicopter/.

[vii] Schächtele, Kai. "Flying Towards a Fossil Fuel-Free Future: The HY4." Wired UK. December 01, 2016. Accessed December 03, 2016. http://www.wired.co.uk/article/zero-emission-plane.

[viii] Winter, Lumen, and Glenn Degner. Minute Epics of Flight. New York: Grossett & Dunlap, 1933.

[ix] "Petroczy PKZ I." All the World's Rotorcraft. 2008. Accessed November 27, 2016. http://www.aviastar.org/helicopters_eng/petroczy-pkz.php.

[x] Taylor, John W. R. Jane's All the World's Aircraft: 1974-75. Vol. 1. London: Jane's Yearbooks, 1974.

[xi] "Silent Club Electric Self-Launch Sailplane." AliSport. 2002. Accessed November 27, 2016. http://www.alisport.com/eu/eng/silent_b.htm.

[xii] Bremner, Charles. "Air Travel Switches to Electricity." The Times (London), January 3, 2008. January 3, 2008. Accessed November 26, 2016.

[xiii] Koehler, Tom. "A Green Machine." Boeing Frontiers, May 2008.

[xiv] Paur, Jason. "Chip Yates Sets 5 New Electric Plane World Records in 4 Weeks." Wired. October 13, 2013. Accessed November 28, 2016. https://www.wired.com/2013/10/yates-world-records/.

[xv] Harbaugh, Jennifer. "Green Flight Challenge." STMD: Centennial Challenges. July 8, 2016. Accessed December 16, 2016. https://www.nasa.gov/directorates/spacetech/centennial_challenges/general_aviation/index.html.

[xvi] Wells, Douglas. "NASA Green Flight Challenge: Conceptual Design Approaches and Technologies to Enable 200 Passenger Miles per Gallon." 11th AIAA Aviation Technology, Integration, and Operations (ATIO) Conference, April 20, 2011. doi:10.2514/6.2011-7021.

[xvii] Robinson R44 Raven II Pilot's Operating Handbook and FAA Approved Rotorcraft Flight Manual. Torrance, CA: Robinson Helicopter Company, 2005.

[xviii] Kallo, Josef. "HY4 - Zero-emission Passenger Flights." Institute of Engineering Thermodynamics - HY4. November 26, 2015. Accessed December 16, 2016. http://www.dlr.de/tt/en/desktopdefault.aspx/tabid-10743/.

[xix] Palt, Karsten. "Cessna 172 Skyhawk - Specifications - Technical Data / Description." Flugzeug Info. 2016. Accessed December 16, 2016. http://www.flugzeuginfo.net/acdata_php/acdata_cessna172_en.php.

[xx] "The Right Choice for the Large Airplane Market." Startup. May 2010. Accessed December 16, 2016.

http://www.boeing.com/resources/boeingdotcom/company/about_bca/startup/pdf/historical/747-400-passenger.pdf.

[xxi] "Battery." Oxford Dictionary. 2016. Accessed December 2, 2016.

[xxii] Finn, Bernard S. "Origin of Electrical Power." Powering A Generation: Power History. 2014. Accessed December 02, 2016. http://americanhistory.si.edu/powering/past/prehist.htm.

[xxiii] Calvert, James B. "The Electromagnetic Telegraph." The Electromagnetic Telegraph. June 1, 2004. Accessed December 04, 2016. http://mysite.du.edu/~jcalvert/tel/morse/morse.htm.

[xxiv] Gaston "Gaston Plant (1834-1889)." Corrosion Doctors. 2010. Accessed December 04, 2016. http://www.corrosion-doctors.org/Biographies/PlantelBio.htm.

[xxv] "Comparison of Battery Types." Wikipedia. 2016. Accessed December 04, 2016. https://en.wikipedia.org/wiki/Comparison_of_battery_types.

[xxvi] (Electric 2016) "Electric Jumbo Jets: How Many Batteries Do You Need to Get Airborne?" Battery Bro. March 22, 2016. Accessed December 04, 2016. https://batterybro.com/blogs/18650-wholesale-battery-reviews/98659398-electric-jumbo-jets-how-many-batteries-do-you-need-to-get-airborne.

[xxvii] Schweber, Bill. "Lithium Batteries: The Pros and Cons.",Electronics360. August 4, 2015. Accessed December 04, 2016. http://electronics360.globalspec.com/article/5555/lithium-batteries-the-pros-and-cons.

[xxviii] ibid.

[xxix] "Pack Safe: Lithium-Ion and Lithium Metal Batteries." Federal Aviation Administration. March 19, 2015. Accessed December 4, 2016. https://www.faa.gov/about/initiatives/hazmat_safety/more_info/?hazmat=7.

[xxx] (Battery 2006 "Battery Statistics." Battery University. 2006. Accessed December 04, 2016. http://batteryuniversity.com/learn/archive/battery_statistics.

[xxxi] Khurmi, R. S., and R. S. Sedha. Materials Science. New Delhi: S. Chand, 2008.

[xxxii] Ayrton, W. E. Practical Electricity. London: Cassell &, 1892 ,pg 183-185.

[xxxiii] "Graphene Supercapacitors vs. Hydrogen Fuel Cells." BTE Blog. March 23, 2013. Accessed December 05, 2016. http://www.buildtheenterprise.org/graphene-supercapacitors-vs-hydrogen-fuel-cells.

[xxxiv] "Biking to Work Increases 60 Percent Over Last Decade." The United States Census Bureau. May 08, 2014. Accessed December 05, 2016. http://www.census.gov/newsroom/press-releases/2014/cb14-86.html.

[xxxv] "Carbon Emissions from Aircraft and Ships." A Response to Climate Change. 2015. Accessed December 05, 2016. http://petrolog.typepad.com/climate_change/2009/09/carbon-emissions-from-aircraft-and-ships.html.

CHAPTER 2:

LIGHTER, FASTER, STRONGER

THE FUTURE OF AVIATION MATERIALS

Gary Gates, Junior

Bioengineering

History of Wooden Airplanes

Airplanes were not always the hulking metal behemoths that we now know. The origin of the airplane is a modest one, constructed of light woods and fabric in order to allow these infantile contraptions to get lift off the ground. With engine technology in an early state of development, airplanes required very high strength-to-weight ratios in order to maintain flight. Except for engineers like Hiram Maxim and Samuel Langley, who attempted to make metal-based airplanes but were largely unsuccessful, most of the early airplane makers shied away from metal materials. Metals and other heavy materials were cast aside in the early 1900s due to their immense weight. With airplane technology being so young and unexplored, it was more important for the inventors to focus their efforts on getting lift and sustaining flight, rather than focusing on the problems that would occur later, such as durability and strength, where metals would succeed. Below is a timeline for a brief summary of the topics that this chapter will touch on.

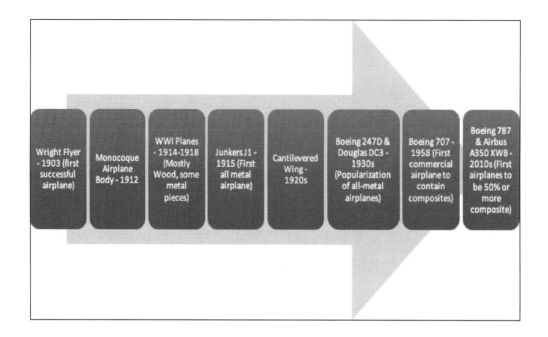

The very first controlled airplane to sustain flight rather than gliding was the Wright brothers' Flyer, which was flown in 1903 and mostly made out of giant spruce wood[i]. The construction of the Wright Flyer was fairly new for its time and featured wings with two thin strips of ash separated by blocks, rather than the steam-bent ribs that were prominent in the gliders that came before the Wright Flyer. In order to create a more aerodynamic wing the Wright brothers covered the underside of the wooden frame of the wings with layers of fabric. This fabric gave the bottom of the wing a smooth and rounded figure. The wing was then covered with another fabric pocket, that was sewn to the bottom fabric layer, which allowed the wooden structure of the wing to float inside the fabric pocket. This fabric helped further improve the smoothness of the wing and thus increased the aerodynamic efficiency of the airplane.

Even though World War I helped the advancement of airplanes, the selection of airplane materials did not advance much until the First World War had passed. The majority of aircraft advancement during the war came from engine improvements and stabilization improvements in order to help the airplanes fly more efficiently and precisely. Even the aircraft that is often referred to as the best of World War I, the Fokker D-VII, did not feature much in terms of material advancement. The D-VII was, like most planes of its time period, still being built of wood and covered in canvas and other fabrics for smoothness and protecting the wooden structure[ii].

One of the first great advancements to aviation was the monocoque configuration. The monocoque was developed in 1911 by Eugene Ruchonnet in order to eliminate the need for an internal skeleton in the fuselage of an airplane. In place of this skeleton, the skins, which were thin layers of wood or plywood, of the airplane were glued on top of each other in a crossing pattern to take stress in multiple directions. The skin therefore functioned as the structure of the airplane, as it would take the stress for the weight of the plane. The monocoque was a great step in aircraft structural design but did have its flaws, namely weight and structural problems. Eventually, as the size of an airplane increases, a monocoque shell will reach the point where it weighs more than would a typical internal skeleton. This means that a monocoque design can be beneficial for smaller airplanes, but loses the weight advantage when it comes to larger aircraft. Another disadvantage of the monocoque is that it, being one shell, can have its structural integrity ruined with one structural failure.

One of the first airplanes to make real use of the monocoque design was the Deperdussin Monocoque, an early racing aircraft designed by Louis Béchereau in 1912. The Deperdussin Monocoque was a monoplane, meaning it had only one pair of wings, which was a still growing trend. This trend was more popular in racing airplanes than fighter planes, which were at the time much more commonly biplanes than monoplanes. The wings of the Deperdussin Monocoque were made of hickory and ash for the ribs and pine for the spars. The fuselage for this airplane was made of tulipwood and hickory. Due to the light weight design of the monocoque, pilots flying the Deperdussin Monocoque were able to win many competitions in the early 1910s[iii].

The response to the monocoque's downfalls was the semi monocoque design, which is still the most common fuselage design to this day for metal skinned aircraft and in general aviation. The semi monocoque is a hybrid of the monocoque and the full-load-bearing internal skeleton. In the semi monocoque the fuselage is supported by a partial internal skeleton to help support the skin. The semi monocoque allows the skin and internal skeleton to share the weight of the airplane, which turned out to be a happy compromise between the two structural designs, so much so that even though it has certainly been improved it has not entirely been redesigned or replaced.

While the fuselage is one important point of airplane design and structure, another element of the aircraft that needed redesign was the airplane wing. The first functioning airplane designs were generally externally braced. This meant that the airplanes would have multiple pairs of wings, which were supported by wooden struts and wires to take stress. An important advancement to wooden airplanes was the development of the cantilevered wing. Instead of the aforementioned externally braced wings, the cantilever relied on no bracing or struts. The spar on the cantilevered wing was self-supporting and provided strength for the entire wing[iv]. Another advantage of the cantilevered wing is that it is connected directly to the plane's fuselage, which improves the plane's structure, rigidity, and stress-bearing. The cantilevered wing, especially in its youth, was often covered with fabric, however, as airplane technology progressed, fabric was quickly exchanged for a wooden skin. Inventors and manufacturers found that they could substitute light woods in as the airplane skin as the wood would bear loads better and was more durable than the fabrics. Wing construction and design saw frequent redesign and improvement from the early externally braced wing design in the 1910s to the cantilevered wing that gained traction later in the 1920s and 1930s. A parallel in wing development can also be seen later in the improvement of the metal wing, as will be discussed shortly[v].

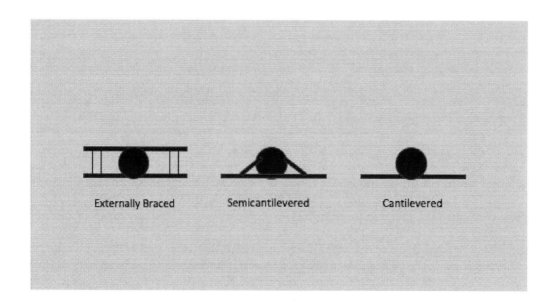

Externally Braced   Semicantilevered   Cantilevered

History of Metal Airplanes

As airplane technology improved, inventors and manufacturers gained the ability to explore materials other than wood. While wood was a good starting point for airplane development due to its light weight and thus the fact that it required lower engine output to achieve lift, the advantages of metal were too large to overlook. Although metal was tested and used in airplanes in the 1910s, it took until the 1930s for metals to become a prominent force in the aircraft industry.

One of the first successful inventors to experiment with metals in aviation was Anthony Fokker. Fokker made airplanes for the Germans in World War I and tested metals as substitutes for the wooden parts in the box-girder fuselages of his cantilevered airplanes. These planes were not metal monocoques, but still proved that metal could be used effectively in airplanes.

The first successful all metal airplane was the Junkers J1, which was built out of sheet steel in 1915[vi]. The J1 was a great first step for metal aviation as it demonstrated that airplanes could function and achieve appropriate lift with heavier materials, like steel, but certainly had its fair share of problems. First and foremost, the J1 was heavy and had very little maneuverability. It was also incredibly slow due to its heavy and unrefined choice of metal. Despite these downfalls it gave way to the popularization of metal aircrafts, which boomed only fifteen years after its birth.

The two airplanes that finally brought metals to the forefront of airplane engineering in the 1930s were the Boeing 247D and the Douglas DC3. The Boeing 247D, constructed in 1933, was a cantilevered monoplane built entirely out of anodized aluminum. It is to this day considered the first fully metal semi monocoque aircraft and, for this reason, it is often referred to as the first modern airplane. Aluminum was a much better metal for the fuselage of airplanes than sheet steel, previously used in the J1, mostly due to the fact that it is sturdy but much lighter than steel. The wings of the 247 each had one heavy spar that supported the wings' load. They were covered in sheet metal for rigidity. The 247 was used until World War II, when it was replaced with airplanes that improved on its design.

The Douglas DC3 was another all metal monoplane developed in 1936 that had a profound effect on metal aircraft design and manufacturing. One of the most revolutionary things about the DC3 was that it had multi-cellular wings. While many planes in the time period featured a single heavy spar, like that of the 247, a design that links all the way back to Fokker's monoplane designs in World War I, the DC3 had many smaller spars that intersected with the wings metal ribs to create small cells in the wing. These cells were covered with sheet metal by riveting the sheet metal directly over the top of the cells. This multi-cellular design allowed the DC3 to carry a larger wing load than the 247[v].

Due to metal's strength advantages over wood, it quickly took off in aviation design. While aluminum has been the primary discussed topic due to its common usage in airplane fuselages and wings, there are also other airplane metals worth mentioning. Aluminum's main advantages are its high strength-to-weight ratio and its corrosion resistance[vii], which is why it is used as a frequent body part of airplanes.

Steel has higher tensile strength than aluminum and also has a higher elastic modulus. These two advantages cause manufacturers to use steel frequently in landing gear. Titanium is another important metal to aviation and is used in building airplane engines. Nickel-based super-alloys are often used in combination with titanium in engines due to their heat and corrosion resistance[viii].

Due to their strength and durability, metals have been and continue to be popular in airplanes. They are very durable, which is an important property for any sort of vehicle transporting people and important goods. While technology has changed in aviation and metals have been improved, the common usage of metals has not changed to an extreme degree. As opposed to the choice of physical materials used in airplanes, more effort has been placed in improving engines, airplane shape, and achieving drag reduction. Metals appear to be here for the long run, with the only threat looming on the horizon being the increasing development and usage of composites.

Composite Aviation

Composite materials started to be used in aircrafts in the 1970s, but were not used in significant quantities until the early 2000s. As a whole, composites are still a largely immature material in the world of aviation, but certainly show promise, as indicated with their recent growth and upward trend of usage.

The main composites that will be discussed in this chapter are fiber-reinforced polymers (RFPs). FRPs, like fiberglass and carbon fiber, are the most frequently used type of composite material. An FRP usually consists of a polymer matrix that has been reinforced with fibers. The most commonly used fibers in aviation are glass, carbon, aramid and basalt. The polymer used in a composite is usually an epoxy, a vinyl-ester, or a polyester.

The main advantages to using composites over metals are weight and corrosion resistance. Decreasing weight in airplanes is one of the quickest and easiest ways to increase efficiency, which is vital in decreasing consumption and saving money. Increased resistance to corrosion, on the other hand, helps maintain the structural integrity of an airplane, therefore keeping planes active and up in the air. Other advantages of composites are the flexibility of the material and their multi-directionality, meaning their ability to be woven in many crossing directions. Flexibility has many important contributions to airplanes, specifically being able to bear loads in the correct region of an airplane or allowing wings to flex along their span, increasing efficiency. The weave of composites can also be crossed in order to increase stiffness in multiple or specific directions, which is also important for load bearing in airplanes[ix,x].

The first prominent commercial airplane to make use of composites was the Boeing 707. The 707, which took its first flight 1958, contained two percent fiberglass by mass[xi]. The rest of the airplane industry did not make frequent use of composites until the 1970s. The 707 was one of the first jet airliners to be commercially viable, but also saw cargo and military applications and derivatives, such as a freighter model and reconnaissance and transport derivatives. The Boeing 707 was, like most airplanes before it and the majority of airplanes to follow it, made mostly of aluminum alloys. However, Boeing decided to use approximately 20 square meters of fiberglass in the 707's cabin structure. Although this was a minor addition of composite to a tertiary structure of an airplane, Boeing's actions introduced the idea of adding composites to commercial airplanes in order to save weight in any places possible. Less weight is more efficiency, and even small weight differences can make large efficiency savings.

The Airbus A310, which was introduced in 1982, was the next airplane to advance composite usage. The A310 and subsequent A300 both used approximately 5% composite material by mass, a 3% increase by mass from the 1958 Boeing 707. However, as opposed to the fiberglass that was used in the Boeing 707, the A310 and A300 used carbon fiber, and used this carbon fiber in larger structural parts of their airplane. Airbus replaced the typical metal structure of the vertical stabilizers with carbon fiber materials to achieve significant weight savings. The approximate size of the vertical stabilizer is 8.3 meters by 7.8 meters at the base, which equates to a much larger region of composite used on the A310 when compared to the 707. While helping the aviation industry make composites more commonplace in aircraft, Airbus also achieved a large weight saving in replacing their stabilizer with carbon fiber. At the time, a standard aluminum alloy stabilizer weighed 400 kilograms more than its carbon fiber counterpart. This weight saving led to a 0.5 percent reduction in fuel burnt per hour, which although not an incredibly large number, is still a significant saving, especially considering all the money spent on fuel for commercial airliners. Composites were also used on floor struts and panels, spoilers, and landing gear doors, which added up to even more weight savings[11].

Airbus' next uses of composite materials were with its A340 and A380. The A340, which made its first flight in 1993, featured 10 percent composite material by mass. It shared similar features to Airbus' A300, like the carbon fiber stabilizer, but also used composites in its spoilers and other regions. Airbus increased its commercial airliner composite composition to approximately 25 percent composites by mass with the A380 in 2005. As Airbus moved to newer models, they also started to phase out their use of glass composites in favor of higher usage of carbon fiber composites. At the same time, Airbus also introduced a new material to its airplanes, which they coined as GLARE, or glass laminate aluminum reinforced epoxy. GLARE consists of a fiber metal laminate, such as very thin sheets of aluminum interspersed with glass fiber, bonded with a matrix of epoxy[xii]. GLARE shares many commonalities with traditional aluminum, and although it is technically a composite, GLARE, in terms of its physical properties, is much closer to traditional aluminum alloy. GLARE's advantages over aluminum alloys are its damage tolerance, corrosion resistance, fire resistance, and lower specific weight. In its A380, Airbus used Glare in the front and rear portions of the fuselage and used carbon fiber composites in its ailerons, flaps, engine cowlings, and its vertical and horizontal stabilizers. Overall, Airbus' conversion to composite materials led to approximately a 16.5 ton savings in weight.

While they did not introduce any groundbreaking new composite materials to commercial airliners like Airbus, Boeing created its 777 in 1995, which was 12 percent composite material by mass[xiii]. Some composite features of the 777 are the edge panels and fairings, which contained fiberglass, and the flaps, ailerons, rudders, elevators, and cowlings, which contained carbon composites.

Both Boeing and Airbus took a huge leap forward with composites in the twenty-first century, vaulting their new commercial airliners into the 50-percent-or-more composite by mass range. Boeing took the bold step first, and introduced the 787 Dreamliner in 2011. The 787 is approximately 50 percent composite material by mass, which equates to approximately 80 percent composite material by volume. The rest of the plane is consisted of 20 percent aluminum, 10 percent steel, 15 percent titanium and 5 percent of other material by mass. Boeing stated that the conversion to using composites as the primary material of the airliner allowed them a 20 percent weight saving when compared to a conventional aluminum airliner, which saves a great deal of fuel in the long run[xiv]. The primary uses of composites in the 787 are regions of tension, like the fuselage and wings. An interesting change that Boeing made in their metal composition is that they increased the percent composition of titanium. While titanium is generally heavier than aluminum, it is lower maintenance, handles compression loads better, and better for the environment than aluminum. Titanium is used in regions like the engine pylon in order to handle compressive forces.

The Airbus A350 XWB only slightly ousts the 787 in terms of composite material percentage, sporting 53 percent composite materials by mass composition. In terms of other materials, however, Airbus' A350 is very similar to the 787. The A350 is 14 percent titanium by mass, 7 percent steel, and 19 percent aluminum. Also similar to the 787, the A350 utilizes most of its composite material (carbon fiber composites) in its fuselage and wings[xv]. Another shared component between the two planes is the flexed shape of the wings. Thanks to the flexible abilities of carbon fiber composites, both Airbus and Boeing were able to tilt their wings and therefore increase the curvature of the wings. There is a slight difference in where each company added curvature to their wings. Airbus flexed the tip of their wing up to an approximately 90 degree angle, which, according to Airbus, leads to a faster, more efficient, and quieter aircraft. Boeing, on the other hand, increased the overall curvature of their wing and flexed the tip up to a lesser extent. While Boeing claimed a 20 percent increase in efficiency in comparison to an all-aluminum model, Airbus claims a 25 percent increase in efficiency compared to an aluminum counterpart, likely as a result of its lower usage of metals.

While composite materials like glass fiber reinforced polymers and carbon reinforced polymers have a lot of obvious benefits, such as lighter specific weight, better flexibility, better corrosion resistance, and better damage tolerance, composites are not without their drawbacks. First and foremost, composites are an expensive technology[xvi]. This of course is subject to change as composite technology matures and composites get more exposure; the price of technology tends to decrease as the popularity of the product increases. This, however, does not change the fact that the current startup cost to building an airplane with aluminum is much less than building one with composites. Another glaring issue with composites is the way they take damage. When an aluminum body on an airplane has taken damage it is usually very obvious, seeing as the metal will dent and show signs of stress. Composites on the other hand do not damage as easily as metal but also do not show signs of internal damage on their exterior[xvii]. This means that the body of a composite airplane could be compromised without obviously showing this to engineers, making maintenance a potentially risky or tedious process. Finally, composites also have a problem with heating. Because popular composites are suspended in epoxies and polymers, they do not have as high of heat resistance as would a typical aluminum alloy.

Current composite technology is therefore much more difficult to use in jet engines and other exceedingly hot regions of an airplane. Not only is there the potential possibility that composites change form or melt in hot temperatures, there is also the possibility that, since many composites are resin-based, a composite pushed past its heat threshold emits toxic fumes. It is important for aircraft manufacturers to evaluate the advantages and disadvantages of composites to decide whether the increasing usage of composites in place of aluminum is worth it on aircraft. Engineers will also continue to redesign composites to improve their physical properties and engineer new materials, such as superalloys and ceramic composites that will be discussed in the upcoming section.

Future Materials and Forecasting

There is a lot of promise on the horizon for new and developing material technologies in airplanes. While aluminum alloy has been a major force on the market, the winds have been singing songs of change, as FRP composite technology has increased recently at an astounding rate, and as a result, other viable alternatives, such as superalloys and alternative composites are getting notice as well. In this section these new and expanding technologies and concepts will be examined and forecasts will be made concerning what will be seen in the future.

While composite's recent jump may seem like the type of technological leap that will taper off or only last for a short time, many aviation experts and researchers believe that composites are still in the development stage and still have an immensely large potential for further growth and development. As evidence for the looming potential of composite growth, NASA, the FAA, and various other aviation-focused organizations recently signed a partnership to extend the research into composites on April 2, 2015[xviii]. Named "NASA's Advanced Composites Project," this partnership aims to increase the rate at which composite materials are adopted into aviation. The partnership selected the National Institute of Aerospace in Hampton, Virginia to oversee the Advanced Composites Consortium, which will work to better composites research and the certification of composites. This effort will ideally bring composites to the market at a quicker rate and give those researching composites more help and guidance in order to improve current composite knowledge and technology.

While FRP composites like carbon fiber are currently at the forefront of composite, they are still constantly being redesigned and improved. One such example is MIT's current research on carbon composites, which involves incorporating nanotubes into composites for damage control. As was discussed earlier, one of the problems with carbon composites is that there is no dent to carbon composites when they are damaged, but there may be internal damage that is unseen to the naked eye. There are ways of examining this damage, the most common being using infrared thermography technology to heat the composite and evaluate thermographic images. If there are cracks in the composite, heat will be redirected and will be visible to the camera. This procedure, however, necessitates the use of very bulky equipment and is thus rather difficult. MITs solution in incorporating nanotubes in the composites allows the thermographic imaging of composite material without needing to heat up the composite. Instead, all that is needed is electrical current to pass through composite, which is a much easier process than heating up the aircraft as it can be accomplished with a handheld device[xix]. Solutions like this for composite's major problems are what composite technology needs in order to keep up its rapid expansion.

Another new group of composites that could be seeing their way into commercial airplanes in the near future are ceramic matrix composites, or CMCs. While one of the major flaws with typical carbon composite FRPs are their physical heat properties and lack or heat resistance, CMCs work much better with high temperatures. Rather than the having fibers suspended in a polymer, like an FRP, CMCs have ceramic fibers embedded in a ceramic matrix. General Electric is a current leader in CMC research and recently opened the first American CMC plant in Asheville, North Carolina in 2015. This plant will increase the production of CMCs in America, working alongside the two existing CMC "lean labs" that GE already operates in Newark, Delaware and Cincinnati, Ohio. The CMCs that GE is making, or 'super ceramics' as they are coining them, are as durable as metals but can operate at 2,400 degrees Fahrenheit, which is 500 degrees higher than typical metals. These ceramics allow engines to burn much more efficiently at much higher temperatures. GE even believes that CMCs could yield a 25 percent increase in thrust and 10 percent increase in efficiency for modern jet engines by 2020. While this technology has not yet been used in commercial airplanes, it has been proven viable in other settings. GE has already used ceramic composite shrouds in gas turbines, meaning that the turbines are functioning without flaw in the hottest parts of these engines. The current process underway with GE's CMCs is the testing of the ceramic composite shrouds in the new GE9X engine, which is being designed for use in future builds of the Boeing 787. GE foresees a dramatic increase in the demand for CMC parts after the GE9X engine is completed and used in new airplanes in 2020[xx].

As demand for composites increases but the price for these composites remains higher than most metal materials, it is only natural for metal manufacturers to fight back. One such example is Alcoa, a company working out of Pittsburg, Pennsylvania that is known for its lightweight metal manufacturing. One of Alcoa's most promising new technologies is its aluminum-lithium alloy. While most aluminum alloys in airplanes are made with copper, magnesium, manganese, silicon, tin, or zinc as their alloying metal, Alcoa's lightweight aluminum takes advantage of lithium's low density (it is the least dense of all metals) to create a metal that is competitively light when compared to composites. Alcoa even claims that an airplane built with their aluminum lithium alloy is 10 percent lighter than one built intensively with composite materials. Alcoa's aluminum alloy has certainly seen some success to this point, and has allowed the company to create large partnerships with both Boeing and GE[xxi]. Another metal that Alcoa is known for is its nickel-based superalloy. A superalloy that has higher heat resistance than a typical alloy, and also features advanced mechanical strength, surface stability, and corrosion resistance. GE will be using Alcoa's superalloy as airfoils, or turbine blades, for its jet engines and gas turbines while Boeing will be using Alcoa's aluminum alloy for its wing skins on metal airplanes and future 787s[xxii]. The technological improvement of metals, which are generally much cheaper than their composite counterparts, is valuable to the material advancement of aviation as a whole. The quest to make, cheaper, stronger, lighter, and better materials will be increasingly helpful to aircrafts as manufacturers keep trying to build more efficient airplanes.

Materials of the Future

What will your grandchildren see when they look up in the sky? In order to answer this question it is vital to understand technological trends and to examine history. As history has repeatedly demonstrated, most new technologies take time to develop in their earlier years. It took time for wooden airplanes to find their shape and form, but once they caught on new designs and shapes, like the cantilevered plane and the semi monocoque fuselage were developed and stuck, until design and technology began to taper off. However, as wooden airplane technology began to slow down, metal airplane technology was having its own development and then its own renaissance. It followed its trajectory to the same end as wood, and decelerated until only slow changes were being made in aluminum, titanium and steel technology. The general pattern for technology advancement is known as an 'S curve.' It takes time for a technology to develop, slowly gaining acceptance and enticing more and more people into researching its potential. As researchers explore the technology's every nook and cranny, the technology slowly approaches its limit. For whatever reason it be, exhaustion of ideas, lack of accompanying technology, or overall loss of potential, the technology reaches its limit and phases out, leaving researchers to find the next new thing and ride its potential to new greatness, discoveries, and possibilities.

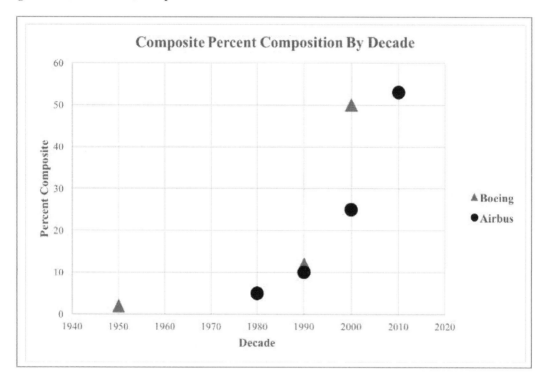

A plot of the percentage of composites by mass in Boeing and Airbus' commercial airliners shows a slow increase in composites from the 1950s through 1990s. Boeing's 707 was 2 percent composite material by mass in 1958 and Airbus' A310 and A300 were 5 percent composite material by mass in the 1970s and 1980s. Both manufacturers saw decent improvements in their percent composite composition in the 1990s, with Airbus reaching 10 percent composite by mass on its A340 in 1993 and Boeing reaching 12 percent composite material by mass on its 777 in 1995. Both companies were testing composites for the most part at this point, keeping the composites in secondary or tertiary features of their airliners. However, with the success that these airliners had, the development and usage of composites rose dramatically to where it is today, with Boeing and Airbus' current commercial models both containing at least 50 percent composite material by mass. While the technology may taper off soon for fiber reinforced polymers like carbon fiber and fiberglass (which already seems to be phasing out) I believe that it is highly unlikely that composites will reach their peak until aircraft manufacturers have experienced more with composite design and implementation, meaning airplanes will still reach higher peak percentages of composite by mass. And while FRP composites may taper off, composite technology as a whole is still largely unexplored and growing. Ceramic matrix composites will certainly grow and see use in the near future, maybe even taking off where carbon fibers left off, serving as better heat resistant materials to create lighter and more efficient aircrafts. In response, metal technology will also improve, meaning that although the mass percentage of aluminum and other metals may still decrease on commercial airliners, it is not likely that these materials will ever be completely removed from aviation. Their cost and simplicity is far too beneficial for them to disappear.

So what will your grandchildren see when they look up at the sky? They will likely see lighter and more efficient airplanes that are a mixture of improved old technologies and the developing technologies like composites that we now know today. As a whole, if I were to make an educated guess on the composition of your average commercial airliner, I would posit that the majority of commercial aircrafts would be at least 50 percent composite material by mass. The engines and other heat-dependent parts will contain ceramic matrix composites while the fuselage and the wings of the airplane will have carbon fiber and other new and developing composites that have been technologically improved in ways similar to the way that MIT has been experimenting with nanotubes in their composites. Metals, though maybe less prominent, will still have their place on commercial airliners. So when your grandchildren look up, they will see engines producing contrails with their superalloy components and other compressive pieces made of improved aluminum lithium alloys. Overall, your children will still see a work in progress, but that is the way that technology will always be. We are always striving to better our materials, methods, and designs and will reach no end because progress is always tempting us on the horizon.

[i] "Inventing a Flying Machine." Smithsonian National Air and Space Museum, Smithsonian. Accessed 18 Dec. 2016.

[ii] "Fokker D.VII." *Smithsonian National Air and Space Museum*, Smithsonian. Accessed 18 Dec. 2016.

[iii] Flannigan, Pat. "Semi Monocoque, Mono-what?" *AviationChatter*, 19 Jan. 2010.

[iv] "Aircraft Structures." *Aviation Maintenance Technician Handbook*, vol. 1, Federal Aviation Administration, 2012, pp. 1-1 - 1-48.

[v] Jakab, Peter L. "Wood to Metal: Structural Origins of the Modern Airplane." *Journal of Aircraft*, vol. 36, no. 6, Nov. 1999, pp. 914-918. *Biomedical Engineering and Mechanics - Virginia Tech.*

[vi] Day, Dwayne A. "Metal-Skinned Aircraft." *Centennial of Flight*, U.S. Centennial of Flight Commission. Accessed 18 Dec. 2016.

[vii] "Materials." *How Things Fly*, Smithsonian. Accessed 18 Dec. 2016.

[viii] Bowler, Tim. "Carbon fibre planes: Lighter and stronger by design." *BBC News*, British Broadcasting Company, 28 Jan. 2014.

[ix] *Future Technology and Aircraft Types*. Stanford University. Accessed 18 Dec. 2016.

[x] Chady, Tariq. "AIRBUS VERSUS BOEING--COMPOSITE MATERIALS : The sky's the limit..." *LeMauricien.com*, Le Mauricien, 6 Sept. 2013.

[xi] Gardiner, Ginger. "The resurgence of GLARE." *CompositesWorld*, 18 Aug. 2016.

[xii] Tenek, Lazarus Teneketzis, and John Argyris. *Finite Element Analysis for Composite Structures*. Springer-Science+Business Media, B.V., 1998. *Google Books.*

[xiii] "Boeing 787: From the Ground Up." *Boeing*. Accessed 18 Dec. 2016.

[xiv] "A350 XWB: Technology." *Airbus*. Accessed 18 Dec. 2016.

[xv] Michaels, Daniel. "Their New Materials." *The Wall Street Journal*, 17 June 2013.

[xvi] Houston, Sarina. "Advantages and Disadvantages of Composite Materials on Airplanes." *the balance*, About.com, 31 July 2015.

[xvii] Northon, Karen. "NASA Creates Partnership to Advance Composite Materials for Aircraft of the Future." *NASA*, National Aeronautics and Space Administration, 4 May 2016.

[xviii] Leonard, Frank. "New advanced composite material lends itself to aircraft safety." *New Atlas*. Accessed 11 Apr. 2011.

[xix] Kellner, Tomas. "Space Age Ceramics Are Aviations' New Cup Of Tea." *GE Reports*, General Electric, 13 July 2016.

[xx] Oravecz, John D. "Alcoa signs $1B contract with Boeing for aluminum aircraft products." *TribLIVE*, 11 Sept. 2014, 11:09 a.m

[xxi] Standridge, Michael. "Aerospace materials -- past, present, and future." *Aerospace: Manufacturing and Design*, 13 Aug. 2014

[xxii] 22 Standridge, Michael. "Aerospace materials -- past, present, and future." *Aerospace: Manufacturing and Design*, 13 Aug. 2014.

CHAPTER 3:

WHO OR WHAT WILL BE YOUR PILOT?

THE FUTURE OF AUTONOMY

Amita Kashyap, Senior

Bioresource Research: Genomics/Bioinformatics

The annual Oregon International Air Show hosted by the Hillsboro Airport in Oregon is a summer highlight for the community. Every year, people come to explore aircraft – vintage, cutting-edge, and everything in between – marvel at the aerial acrobatics, and meet the pilots.
Pilots have long captured the imagination of the public. The flying aces of World War I and World War II were celebrated for their heroics. During the 1920s, the public marveled at the barnstormers, who did daredevil stunts on and in their aircraft – including stunts such as jumping from one plane to another while in the air.[16] Pilots like Charles Lindbergh and Amelia Earhart inspired the public as they broke records and pushed airplanes to go farther, faster, and longer, reaching new heights both literally and metaphorically. As passengers took to the air, the pilot – quite literally – became the respected Captain of the Ship.

These captains command ships that sail not at sea but on the wings of the wind. From the moment they walk past the passengers at the terminal through the gate with the crew – crisply dressed, walking with purpose and a smile on their face – to the moment they smilingly say "Thank you" to the last customer to disembark, they are in command, responsible for the safety of their passengers and making their passengers feel that way. They let children peek in on the cockpit and show them the controls, happy to see the delight on their faces when they are shown around. They greet the passengers between taxi and takeoff, welcoming the guests and orienting them about their journey. They "thank you for flying with us" and "wish you a pleasant stay and safe rest of your trip". They even welcome you home.

But will our grandchildren enjoy these same pleasures that we have been privileged to enjoy? With self-driving cars taking to the streets and computers already active partners in the flying of commercial passenger aircraft, are the days of personable fellow humans taking us places coming to an end?

Come thirty-five years from now, who – or what – *will* be our pilot?

In this chapter, we explore the possibilities, starting with how we came to where we are today, and then asking the question "where are we going". What will it take to fully automate aircraft and banish the familiar pilot and co-pilot from the cockpit? Or will they even bid farewell to the cockpit at all?

A Little History... How We Came To Where We Are Today

Flight deck automation – the computerization of flight controls – is a logical next step from instrumentation in the cockpit, something which became inevitable once pilots understood that they could not rely on their senses and intuition for flying in all weather conditions. On a clear day, a pilot cannot help but see the Earth. If the area is familiar, they can know exactly where they are just by looking at the scene below. And they can easily tell if the plane is tilted and in which direction simply by looking at the horizon, and correct that tilt as necessary. But what if it is dark outside? During the 1920's, electric and gas-powered beacons were set up across the United States to act as lighthouses for pilots. Since a pilot was never out of visual range of a beacon, which were always within roughly ten miles of each other, a pilot could safely fly through the night, as long as s/he followed the lighted path below.[16] But introduce clouds into the sky, and neither the light of the beacons nor the light of day is going to help make heads or tails of the situation. And, it turns out, neither are the pilot's senses.

The inner ear provides the sense of balance, which enables one to perceive spinning and tilting. Though it works great in day-to-day life on the ground, it can easily fool you in the air. William Charles Ocker, army pilot[21] and "Father of Instrument Flying",[25] learned this truth from his doctor in 1926.[21] The experiment was simple: the doctor had Ocker close his eyes and interpret his sensations while being spun in a chair. The results were unnerving: when the chair first began to spin, Ocker correctly identified the direction of the spin. But when the chair slowed down, Ocker felt like he had stopped spinning, and when the chair stopped, he sensed that he had begun to spin in the opposite direction. Ocker realized an important truth thanks to the doctor's little demonstration. He had hit upon the reason pilots so easily spiraled out of control in banked turns,[21] which is when a plane tilts – or "banks" – in a particular direction and consequently turns in that direction. "Flying by the seat of their pants"[21, 25, 26], pilots were misjudging their turns; and trusting their instincts more than whatever instruments they may or may not have been using, they let their inner ears fool them into plunging headfirst into the ground.[21]

So, left to their own (biological) devices, pilots not only can't be sure where they are geographically, but also can't be sure of their orientation spatially.

The solution to the geographic location problem was relatively simple. As long as the pilot knew how to use a map and compass, they were fine… Unless they went into an uncontrolled bank (and turn), as army pilot Carl Crane learned in December of 1925, when he got caught in clouds 8,000 feet above the city of Detroit.[21] As his plane began to spiral out of control, his compass became useless. Crane knew that his erratically spinning and jamming compass could even be spinning in the direction opposite than he would expect for a turn in a given direction. This meant that he couldn't rely on the instrument to correctly judge and remedy his spatial orientation. Luckily for him and his passenger (who was a Congressman's son), sufficient visibility returned after dropping under 1,000 feet and Crane was able to save the plane and complete the flight. As visibility returned, Crane saw the Statler Hotel whiz by as the plane practically brushed the top. He recognized that he had avoided a crash by pure luck and, shaken, completed the trip flying "about ten feet high all the way to Toledo, shaking all the way".[21] Crane realized that his compass had failed him in two key areas at the same time. When the plane began to spiral, his compass could not tell him which direction he was going – as in North, South, East, or West – nor could it tell him his spatial orientation. Crane knew that there had to be a better way... and he found his answer four years later in descriptions of a historic flight by Lieutenant James H. Doolittle.[21]

One description of Lieutenant Doolittle's historic flight appeared in a New York Times page one headline:[26]

BLIND PLANE FLIES

15 MILES AND LANDS;

FOG PERIL OVERCOME

Man's greatest enemy in the air, fog, was conquered
yesterday at Mitchell Field when Lt. James H. Doolittle
took off, flew over a fifteen-mile course and landed again
without seeing the ground or any part of his plane but
the illuminated instrument board. The occasion marked
the first instance in which a pilot negotiated a complete
flight while piloting absolutely blind. The demonstration
was more than an exhibition of blind flying and instrument
perfection. It indicated that aviation had perhaps
taken its greatest single step in safety.

During this historic flight, Doolittle made use of then (and currently) standard engine and navigation instruments. In addition, he had at his disposal the Kollsman barometric altimeter, the Sperry artificial horizon, and the Sperry directional gyroscope. First obtained by Doolittle from its namesake and inventor in 1928, the Kollsman barometric altimeter was the most sensitive and precise altimeter of the time, giving precision within a few feet of actual altitude.[26] In fact, it was "20 times more accurate than the standard devices in use".[16] The two Sperry instruments, named for their inventor Elmer Sperry Sr., were actually two applications of the same basic invention: the Sperry gyroscope. They solved both problems of the compass that Crane had encountered at once. The artificial horizon infallibly indicated the plane's orientation with respect to the Earth's horizon, even during extreme banks, thereby solving the problem of the tumbling compass during rolls and uncontrolled turns. The directional gyroscope (aka gyrocompass) replaced the traditional compass for telling direction (North, South, East, and West) This flight of Doolittle's was, in fact, only an official showcase of something he had been doing on a regular basis, both by himself and with his team.[26]

Crane learned about Doolittle's feat when he was an Army flight instructor at a training base in Texas. He managed to convince his resistant superiors to allow him to convert one of the trainer aircraft into an instrument trainer and equipped it with gyroscopes. One day, Ocker (of the spinning chair experiments discussed earlier), wandered into Crane's hangar. The two formed a partnership and set about systematically proving the merits – and advantages over "flying by the seat of the pants" – of instrument flying to a still-skeptical and mistakenly self-confident flying community.[21] Though it may accurately be said that it was Doolittle and his team who first developed instrument flight with precision and reliability, it was Crane and Ocker who brought instrument flying front and center for the flying community. In 1932, they published the first clear analysis of instrument flying, which finally banished the hubris. *Blind Flight in Theory and Practice* finally convinced the flying community of the futility of relying on their senses only and the need for instrumentation.[21]

Figure 1: The cockpit of a World War I aircraft, the SE5 demonstrates early analog instrumentation.
"Flying the SE.5A". *The Vintage Aviator Ltd*. December 14, 2016.
http://thevintageaviator.co.nz/projects/se-5a-reproduction/flying-se5a

With instrumentation came automation, which is the ability to operate independently of direct human control. These developments had, inevitably, begun well before instrumentation became accepted in the mainstream. On June 18, 1914, Lawrence Sperry, son of Elmer Sperry Sr., and his French mechanic and assistant Emil Cachin flew past awestruck Parisian spectators on the wings of their Curtiss C-2,[27, 32] leaving nobody in the cockpit. To the amazement of the audience, even with no pilot at the controls and even with two men on the wings, the plane remained stable, flying along as usual. The team was, in fact, demonstrating the elder Sperry's gyrostabilizer.[32] The gyrostabilizer was actually three gyroscopes, linked to the control surfaces of the plane.[27] The gyroscopes were run by electrical power. Their mechanical links to the control surfaces of the plane physically induced the actions of control necessary to keep the plane stable as the gyroscopes always maintained their balance, and consequently level flight. The plane would not bank unless prompted by the pilot. But as long as the pilot wished to fly straight and level, s/he could fly hands-off, literally leaving the plane to its own devices. The daredevil stunt won Sperry and Cachin the prize for the Concours de la Sécurité en Aéroplane (Airplane Safety Competition).[27] Now, Sperry and Cachin would have to tackle the perhaps more cumbersome task of fitting their mechanical design to the plethora of control actuation methods – the devices for manually controlling the plane – of the day. The flying community inadvertently came to the rescue of Sperry's device when it uniformly adopted the Deperdussin control layout, in which a stick or yoke controls roll and pitch – which is upwards or downwards tilt –and pedals control yaw – which is a horizontal turn to the right or left. This layout remains in use to this day.[27] With the adoption of these uniform standards for the human interface of aircraft control, Sperry's gyrostabilizer became "one size fits all" at no additional design cost for integration into each new aircraft design.[27]

Automation in the modern sense of the word – with computers, instead of humans, managing large parts of the aircraft's functioning – entered aviation in a big way in the 1960s with the space age, when the incorporation of computers into aircraft was truly pioneered. The National Aeronautics and Space Administration (NASA) pushed the limits of reliability and economy of space in computation with IBM contracts for Gemini and MIT contracts for the Apollo missions.[18] These government contracts were focused solely on equipping NASA's space missions, but the partnership with industry spurred progress in the larger field of computer science and engineering. By the early 1970s, digital technology was becoming reliable enough to put into commercial aircraft, to replace their analog counterparts.[37]

By that time, digital equipment was already in use for a number of subsystems. Companies stood to benefit significantly from converting from analog systems to digital computerized systems. The digital systems were lighter and more space-efficient, affording better fuel efficiency, which was especially valued because jet fuel prices were high. Digital systems were also easier to maintain because they were reliable and easy to update via software. Additionally, they were proving easy to troubleshoot.[37]

Furthermore, as air travel became commonplace and airports correspondingly busier, air traffic control took center stage. One example of the major changes that began to materialize is that descents, instead of being long, straight, and gradual, became curved and steep with final approaches as short as one mile, compared to the previous standard of ten miles.[37]

With more than 100 cockpit instruments and controls and new flight techniques to be learned, the demands of piloting increased, but the time available in which to handle those demands remained the same. The aviation community felt that the overall task of flying a commercial aircraft was becoming unreasonably unsafe. With the overall trend towards cost-efficiency and the increasing complexities of flying itself, improving the accuracy of the numerous sensors and devices that had come to inhabit the cockpit and, more importantly, condensing all the raw information they provided, became essential. The answer was found in electronic flight displays.[37]

An electronic flight display shows all the information from all the sensors on a computer screen. That way, the pilot can monitor the whole aircraft by looking at only one place, instead of having to look at each individual sensor. The concept was not entirely new. The technology had been in use by the military since the 1960s. But it was new to civil aviation. NASA, having taken a lead in research and development for civil aviation as the Apollo program came to a close, pioneered the technology.[37]

In the new technology, information from the various sensors was integrated and interpreted. Only the meaningful results, most importantly navigation and spatial orientation, were displayed in an easily-understandable visual format to the pilot. In fact, flight displays were equipped with three options for type of information and display very early on in research and development. One option included displaying the pitch and bank angles necessary to stay on a predetermined flight path, a feat possible only with real-time computation done by an onboard computer system using the digital data from onboard sensors.[37]

Up until the late 1970s, electronic flight displays for civil aviation were purely research devices. The actual development – that is to say, incorporation into industry – began when Boeing engineers, who had participated in the research at Langley as part of an industry-government partnership, returned to Boeing to take over design of Boeing's new aircraft: the Boeing 737. These engineers were eager to incorporate the new technology into their product, but events took a rather sudden turn in 1978 when the airline industry was deregulated. Suddenly, the industry became very competitive and cost – not technological merit – was the sole primary driving factor of business decisions. At its current state of maturity – notably with monochrome displays, which people worried would not be clear enough – and with cost savings that were difficult to quantify, the electronic flight display just did not make the new capitalist standards. Consequently, Boeing had to opt for traditional electromechanical displays on the 737 instead.[37] What ultimately tipped the scale in favor of the electronic flight display for the next generation of aircraft was an ingeniously crafted marketing effort.

NASA held many demonstration flights for pilots and airline representatives using the electronic flight display system, thus proving the utility of the system in flight to the customers. Consequently, the technology became trusted amongst those who would be owning and employing it. Secondly, Boeing, in 1978, began a cost-analysis comparing electromechanical instruments with both monochrome and color electronic flight displays. The conclusion of the cost analysis was that monochrome flight displays might be cheaper than electromechanical instrumentation, and color flight displays only slightly costlier. Now that the technology was trusted and deemed financially viable, the issue that remained was the ease of reading a monochrome versus a color display. The conclusion was that Boeing's customers placed orders for color electronic displays in the new airplanes. The only problem for Boeing now was to develop reliable color displays. At the time, all color displays which could withstand flight conditions did not show very well if there was too much sunlight and all those that were clearly visible in all light conditions were too fragile to withstand the conditions of flight.[37]

Luckily for Boeing, Rockwell International's Collins Air Transport Division solved the problem in partnership with Japanese television manufacturers Toshiba and Mitsubishi, who adapted their television display technology to endure flight conditions. Boeing had color electronic displays in their Boeing 767 and 757.[37]

But perhaps more significant than the electronics in the cockpit itself was the computerization that accompanied it. Computerization enabled the automation of subsystems, taking the burden of these tasks off of the pilots' shoulders. One notable subsystem that was automated is the landing system.[37] This particular automation helped significantly as approaches became more challenging due to the evolving air traffic control issues. Subsystem automation was the first step towards fully-automated aircraft that can fly without any direct human guidance.

The airplane's newfound ability to make adjustments in-flight on its own accord, without the pilot having to intervene, also enabled greater fuel-efficiency as the aircraft responded to environmental conditions in real-time.[37] Nevertheless, automation had its drawbacks from the start. Of concern to pilots and human engineering specialists was the potential for pilots' manual flying skills to deteriorate as they became too reliant on automated subsystems and lost practice flying the plane manually. They worried that this might result in pilots being uncomfortable or unable to safely take over control via manual overrides in case of a malfunction, endangering the lives of everybody onboard.[37]

Where We Are Today

Nowadays, commercial cockpits are an intricate orchestra of man and machine. Computers have become a sort of co-pilot, with the human pilots giving the commands and the computer and automated subsystems taking care of the grunt work, a model oftentimes referred to as the "glass cockpit". Though subsystems are automated, they still have to be easy to monitor and have manual overrides for when the pilots feel it is necessary to take over. The computers take care of a lot, but from gate to gate, the pilots are still very much involved.

Before the engines are even started, the pilots are making sure everything is in order, first adjusting all controls, settings, and movable parts to the correct settings, and then *verifying* this with the pre-flight checklist.[28] The pilots then manually execute taxi and takeoff, which are yet to be fully automated.[7, 14] Once the plane is airborne, the pilots still continue to fly the plane, either manually or, more likely, via the autopilot. In this case, the word "autopilot", which seems to imply that the plane can guide itself, may be misleading. The word "autopilot" is actually short for "automatic pilot", which is defined as "an airborne electronic control system that automatically maintains a preset heading and attitude". "Attitude" refers to the aircraft's orientation around its axes of rotation.[2, 3, 4] This definition gives a much more accurate idea of what is actually happening. The pilots decide what maneuver is to be done – ascent, descent, start cruising, change cruise speed, choose heading or altitude etcetera – and key in the necessary commands into the appropriate system. That subsystem makes the physical adjustments necessary to execute those commands. The autopilot itself does not choose what to do. It does what is necessary in order to do what the pilots choose to do.[29]

If at any point something goes wrong – the autopilot seems to be working in an unexpected or undesirable way, a subsystem fails, flying gets rough for some reason or another – there are more checklists and protocols to be executed, once any immediate emergency is brought under control. Any of the checklists may be brought up electronically on a screen, but there are also always two hardcopies within easy reach, one for the pilot and one for the co-pilot.[28] Furthermore, at any point, the pilots can choose to disengage the autopilot and fly manually.

On a routine commercial flight, the basics of the flight plan are entered into the Flight Management System (FMS) at the very beginning. The plane takes care of all the intermediate steps instead of the pilots deciding each maneuver one at a time. And if the flight plan changes for any reason, the pilots adjust the plan in the FMS and the aircraft proceeds from there.[20]
Finally, the aircraft descends and lands. The aircraft can autoland – that is to say, the plane can land without the pilots manually intervening – but the aircraft cannot turn off the runway and taxi to the gate. That, again, is up to the pilots' manual controls.[10]

The original problems of reliable navigation and spatial orientation have been addressed with inevitably modernized and upgraded versions of Sperry's artificial horizon and gyrocompass, which remain central to the cockpit. The issue of geographic location has been even more precisely resolved with the Global Positioning System (GPS), so it is no longer necessary to – laboriously – install miles upon miles of beacons. In fact, with GPS, it is no longer necessary to see the ground at all, though blinking lights are still used on towers to warn pilots to fly higher (or foolishly risk crash) and airports and runways are still brightly lit for takeoff and landing. The aircraft themselves are also equipped with a myriad of lights that serve a variety of purposes.[30]

The question now becomes:

Is it possible to take the pilot out of the cockpit altogether?

What will it take?

In order for an aircraft to fly itself, three criteria must be fulfilled. One, the aircraft must have all the information necessary to make informed flight decisions. Two, the aircraft must be able to make sense of that data and decide what to do based on that data. Three, the aircraft must be able to translate that decision into actual action.

The first issue – that of data collection – requires first knowledge of what data needs to be collected. Recall the two challenges pilots originally faced: determining geographic location and determining spatial orientation. The automatically flying aircraft still needs the same information in order to execute the same tasks. Geographic location information allows the pilot – human or computer – to determine and adjust the flight plan. Spatial orientation information allows the pilot to execute the maneuvers necessary to adhere to the flight plan and instructions from Air Traffic Control as well as avoid obstacles and ensure a safe and comfortable flight. But there is also a third type of information of which the pilot must be aware: that of the "health" of the plane – that is to say, how the machinery is working... or not working.

Information of this type takes two forms. One is the physical behavior of the plane that those humans onboard can sense, such as turbulence or the sound of the engines. The second is metrics that the humans cannot directly observe. Information of this type includes altitude, air pressure, and wind speed and direction, to name a few. This type of information is collected by sensors and is then displayed in a human-readable format. The Kollsman barometric altimeter was an example of this.

Any one sensor is good for collecting only one type of information. In principle, the application of sensors can be extended to sensing those characteristics mentioned earlier as detectable only by those humans onboard. The challenge here is to design new sensors, each which accurately and reliably collects the information in question – and only the information in question, filtering out background noise.

So the first challenge in developing autonomous aircraft is to decide what data needs collecting and acquiring or developing the corresponding sensors. But what happens if a sensor fails? For sensors gathering critical information – sensors detecting overheating, over- or under-pressurization, or other signals of system failures, for example – redundancy in the form of multiple sensors of that type is necessary. But redundancy will likely also be necessary in other forms, such as gathering redundant metrics so that if all the sensors for one metric fail, the information from the other sensors gathering the redundant metric can still be used to detect the same potential issues.

The second issue – that of data interpretation and subsequent decision making – is a major software challenge. First, the computer must be made to understand the practical meaning of all the raw data it has at its disposal. Second, the computer must be able to make practical decisions based on that understanding. Teaching a computer, for example, what an unusual sound is and what it might mean in a given situation is much more difficult that teaching a human the same. Humans have to their advantage thousands of years of evolution that has honed their ability to learn. Computers don't. Humans are very good at pattern recognition and pattern matching, enabling them to learn by practice and pick up knowledge through experience. For example, through years of flying planes, human pilots will get very much accustomed to what a plane *should* sound like. So when there comes a time that the plane *doesn't* sound like that, they can pick up on it immediately without even trying. Furthermore, they can decide on how to respond even as the situation changes without necessarily being explicitly told how to do so. All the human pilot requires is some initial training and continued practice, and the cognitively agile human brain takes care of the rest.

Computers, on the other hand, need to be painstakingly programmed – explicitly told exactly how to interpret every piece of information and what actions to take in response. If the computer does not know how to interpret some critical information it could lead to a fatal error. A second layer of complexity is that, in order to program the computer to interpret and make action plans based on the information from its sensors, programmers must know how to interpret and make action plans based on that information. This is no small undertaking. The information received by the computer from the sensors is of a numerical form. The programmers would first have to determine what any particular set, range, or pattern of numbers means practically. Then, based on aerodynamics and the mechanics of the aircraft, the programmers would have to determine what the corresponding plan of action is. Finally, all of this would have to be told to the computer in a format that the computer understands. In recent years, artificial intelligence and machine learning have begun to enable computers to learn in ways analogous to humans, thereby alleviating the need to painstakingly find and provide to the computer a definitive way of treating every situation. However, this technology is still nowhere near the level of efficacy required for autonomous aviation.

Complicated though the process may seem – and is – much of it has already been tackled to get the systems to where they are today. But many challenges – such as automating takeoff and navigating the airport on the ground – still remain if the entire flight is to be automated. Furthermore, audiovisual information, arguably the most difficult to automatically process, is still largely the responsibility of the human pilots and therefore remains to be integrated into the automation. Additionally, none of the current systems support automatic decision making such as responding to emergency situations. These are procedures for which human pilots maintain constant training and rely on experience and innumerable checklists.[28] Programming for following checklists may be possible, but programming to allow the system to be able to respond to any unforeseeable situation requires a deep understanding of first principles of aviation on the part of the programmers. Even "routine flights" can be very work intensive and pilots – the experts themselves – often have to do rapid trouble-shooting of multiple issues and improvise,[31] skills that are difficult, if not impossible, to impart to a computer.

The third issue – that of executing the necessary controls – may indeed already be solved with current autopilots. Perhaps one area to which it remains to be extended is takeoff.

Other Factors

However, automating the airplane itself is only part of the puzzle. Aircraft do not operate in isolation and as such the ability to effectively communicate with others is vital. Arguably the most prevalent communication is that with Air Traffic Control (ATC), responsible for coordinating airborne flights and maintaining safe airways. Currently, the pilot communicates with ATC and inputs the necessary adjustments into the computerized systems. Taking the human intermediary out of the loop would mean that ATC and the aircraft computers would have to be able to talk to each other directly.

Currently, ATC is staffed by humans. Replacing the humans in ATC altogether with a completely computerized system would provide the easiest interface for communication between ATC and autonomous aircraft. But that solution brings along with it a whole host of its own problems: technological advances that are not yet here and costly infrastructural changes. On the other hand, enabling communication between ATC and autonomous aircraft without changing ATC's infrastructure requires, at a minimum, speech recognition on the part of the aircraft. Though speech recognition technology is in use today – iPhone's Siri, Window's Cortana, Ford C-Max's command interface – the technology is far from perfect. These interfaces can recognize only very specific commands and also have significant trouble understanding the smorgasbord of accents that humans sport.

Assuming that the level of automation required for aircraft to fly completely pilotless in all, or even most, conditions comes to be – with or without changes in Air Traffic Control – this raises another interesting issue: network security. Currently, planes can be – and are – hijacked by people who board the plane and take over the cockpit controls by force. Automating everything would not save the industry from such events. They would simply take a new form: that of hijacking the computer system. In-depth discussion of the cybersecurity issues in aircraft automation are beyond the scope of this book but can certainly be a major disadvantage to automation if not sufficiently addressed early on. Indeed, even "simple" bugs – or errors – in any part of the software could prove fatal, without any malicious intent required.

Finally, even if – or when – the technology necessary for autonomous aircraft was adequately developed, there are still two factors hindering its adoption: finance and public acceptance.

As illustrated by the rocky start for the electronic flight display in the commercial airline industry, technological merit alone is not enough for companies to adopt a new technology. They must stand to benefit, or at the very least not make a loss. The original financial gains from reduced instrument weight and in-flight adjustments for more energy-efficient flying are unlikely to drastically improve by virtue of further automation. The systems that rendered these benefits are already in place and further improvements would not necessitate further automation. Also, though airliners could potentially save on employee expenses by cutting pilots' jobs, the research and development costs and costs of infrastructural change would most likely outweigh these savings my thousands or even millions-fold. Furthermore, the airliners would not be the only people who'd have to invest in these changes. As earlier discussed, Air Traffic Control infrastructure and airports would have to change too. That is a lot of people to convince to make a change and would also involve, at least in the United States, government and taxpayer money, which has its own politics and strings attached.

Lessons from Autonomous Cars

Speaking of convincing people, airliners must also be able to convince their customers that the technology is safe and worthwhile. Most people derive comfort from knowing that a person is at the controls. Widespread acceptance of a machine being responsible for one's life is hard to predict, but some insight might be drawn from the parallel of autonomous (also known as self-driving) cars, currently in development by companies such as Tesla and Google.

On October 19, 2016, The Tesla Team announced on the company's website that "as of today, all Tesla vehicles produced in [their] factory – including Model 3 – will have the hardware needed for full self-driving capability at a safety level substantially greater than that of a human driver".[36] The announcement goes on to establish the robustness of the technology due to multiple redundant sensor systems. They seek to build the consumers' trust and confidence by outlining a testing plan and demonstrating their commitment to ensuring complete reliability of the systems before actually enabling them in the cars. Tesla manages to make a marketing pitch and build consumers' trust and confidence all in one concise, comprehensible press release. Furthermore, they mention enabling each system on all Tesla cars remotely as the systems pass testing and validation. Tesla claims the benefit that by doing so they will always be keeping their customers on the "cutting-edge" of technology, appealing to people's competitive spirits and "keeping up with the Jones's" attitudes.

Safety is a selling point not only for Tesla, but for Google as well, who also touts its cars' excellent detection systems. Google also claims benefits that appeal to the more sentimental:[15]

> *Aging or visually impaired loved ones wouldn't have to give up their independence. Time spent commuting could be time spent doing what you want to do. Deaths from traffic accidents—over 1.2 million worldwide every year—could be reduced dramatically, especially since 94% of accidents in the U.S. involve human error.*

Google presents self-driving cars as not only a means to safer roads, but also a means to reclaiming control of one's life, a means to reclaiming one's lost time, a means to reclaiming a more fulfilling life.

The airline industry does not have grounds to make more emotionally appealing claims a la Google, unless they manage to make flight times significantly shorter, with which automation is unlikely to help. Neither does the airline industry appear poised to appeal to the "keeping up with the Jones's" spirit as Tesla does. Though the first airlines to bring self-flying aircraft into service might claim a "cutting-edge" advantage for their customers, that more than likely will not be sufficient to overcome humans' fear of flying without a human at the controls. Furthermore, if the industry goes down the route of autonomous aircraft, the club of passengers flying in autonomous aircraft would be anything but exclusive. The claim to safety, on the other hand, could potentially be a viable selling point. Unfortunately, it is mired in controversy.

The claim for improved safety seems easier to make for self-driving cars than it is for self-flying aircraft. An in-depth report from Business Insider Intelligence found that United Kingdom based KPMG "estimates that self-driving cars will lead to 2,500 fewer deaths between 2014 and 2030".[17] The issue of safety in aircraft as far as automation is concerned is more complex than the black and white picture that seems to have been painted for the automobile industry. Numerous independent studies, including a study commissioned by the Federal Aviation

Administration (FAA), have concluded that, though automation has greatly helped aviation,[9] it has also given rise to serious issues. Most aviation industry professionals concede that automation has greatly improved safety over the last 30 years.[9, 22] However, it has also lead to the so-called "automation paradox": the automation has helped significantly lower the crew's workload during simpler procedures, such as climbing and cruising, but it is significantly increasing the workload during more complex procedures, such as take-off, descent, approach, and landing.[12] Hand in hand with the automation paradox is widespread "automation addiction",[9] which refers to pilots' over-dependence on the autopilot and consequent underutilization of their manual flying skills. So not only are crew members spending a majority of their time inputting data and monitoring subsystems, as per the automation paradox, they are simply relying on the automation too much, as per automation addiction.[9] Consequently, not only do they lose practice with manually controlling the aircraft,[1, 9, 12] but they also lose confidence in what skills and judgment they do have, trusting the automation more than may be warranted.[12] This lack of practice, combined with a lack of understanding of how the automation actually works, has led to a number of automation-related crashes.

Two primary reasons for these crashes are that the pilots either did not comprehend what warning systems were telling them or did not understand how to respond to the situation. A third major factor in these crashes is the aircraft not responding the way the pilots expected it to respond.[12, 22] Pilots expecting the plane to respond in one way but the plane actually behaving in another manner is oftentimes linked with "mode confusion", in which pilots lose track of how the automation is working and what information is and isn't being displayed. But even without mode confusion, automation malfunctions have been responsible for thousands of mishaps, both fatal and recovered.[1] Uneventful automation issues – as far as safety goes – receive bad press for the inconvenience they present, case in point United Airlines flights being grounded due to "automation issues" in June of 2015.[19] Of course, crashes have received substantially more press.

One crash that has received a lot of press, but perhaps more in favor of increased automation, is the 2015 Germanwings crash. In that flight, the pilot deliberately flew into the Alps, committing suicide and taking everybody onboard with him. An opinion article in the Los Angeles Times titled "Germanwings crash: No algorithm can stop a pilot bent on killing himself" highlights the fact that human error – and malice – can easily prove fatal, just as aircraft malfunction can.[14] But the fact remains that removing the human does not remove the possibility of system failure. Thus, aircraft safety and the role that automation plays in aircraft safety remains a complicated issue, perhaps un-leverageable by the aviation industry as a selling point for further automation.

One aspect that automobile automation and aviation automation have in common is technological difficulties, both in terms of cost of technology and in terms of technical capability. The automobile industry is dealing with costly sensors, as much as $80,000 in the case of Google (for LIDAR sensor technology).[33] Sensor costs aside, self-driving cars' next major technological challenge is navigating the busy inner-city streets, which people, especially those who aren't used to it, have enough trouble navigating.[11] Similarly, the aviation industry has all the intricacies of the technological advances discussed thus far to negotiate.

A second aspect that the two industries have in common is regulation challenges. Even as technological concerns are addressed, laws and regulations must be adapted and negotiated. In the case of self-driving cars, those are laws pertaining to roadways and licenses. The aviation industry has FAA regulations to be negotiated. The adaptation of laws and regulations is an inherently slow process. As such, it is a barrier to widespread adoption of automation technology even if the government seeks to support the technology's maturation, as is the case in the United Kingdom,[24] for example.

So it appears that the aviation industry is at a significant disadvantage compared to the automobile industry with regards to going autonomous. Not only does the aviation industry face many of the same challenges and disadvantages that the automobile industry does, it also doesn't stand to benefit from the same advantages. Notably, the aviation industry cannot make the emotional appeal for marketing that the automobile industry does and neither does it have the ability to tout safety, at least if consumers are going to judge from their gut reactions to the current publicity. In this regard, the aviation industry could – and likely does – stand to benefit from the progress of the automobile industry as self-driving cars become more widely employed and accepted, warming up the public to the idea of entrusting their life and safe transportation entirely to a machine.

(Speculative) Models for the Future

But, as the road to self-driving cars and the trajectory of automation in aviation thus far have shown, progress is usually incremental. Currently, two models dominate academic thinking with regards to further commercial aircraft automation, either or both of which could serve as stepping stones to fully self-flying aircraft. One model is that of a remote control cockpit. In this model, a human would still be flying the plane, but that human would no longer actually be in the plane. Instead, the pilot would be sitting in some operation room somewhere, communicating with the plane via the airwaves, much like one flies a remote control model airplane. The second model eliminates the human pilot almost altogether. The plane would take care of itself, and a trained flight attendant – an "attendant-pilot" – would step in if a situation escalated to emergency level.[23]

Figure 2: An example of a remote control cockpit. This remote control cockpit at Creech Air Force Base in Nevada is used to command drones. Patterson, T. Who's really flying the plane? *CNN Travel* (2012).

The remote control cockpit has its advantages. One major advantage is that it does not require aircraft to be more automated than they already are. This model keeps the same human-machine dynamic and simply stretches the distance between the two participants. A second major advantage is that planes would no longer have to be designed with space for two people and a human-friendly interface at the front. (Incidentally, the current interface is reportedly *not* user-friendly).[29] The elimination of this design consideration could potentially save on space. However, because the pilots' involvement in actual operation of the aircraft would not change, there would still have to be a pilot and co-pilot for every flight, which airliners could view as a disadvantage because that means personnel costs remain the same. But, if the airplane's automation was increased to a degree such that one pilot was sufficient and their workload was low, airliners could also potentially put one pilot on multiple flights concurrently. Consequently fewer pilots would be taking care of more flights, all without dealing with jetlag. Alert pilots make for safer flying, but humans are also proven to be terrible multi-taskers, so putting one pilot on multiple flights may bode ill for passenger safety. Furthermore, passengers may not even feel comfortable boarding a plane with no pilot onboard. There is a comfort to knowing that whoever is flying the plane shares the same fate as you.[34] So if things are really going down fast, someone – or two someones – upfront is doing everything within their power to save their own life, and the passengers' as well. A pilot on the ground doesn't necessarily have the same stake in saving a flight, no matter how good-hearted or duty-bound they are. Furthermore, the pilot on the ground is limited by the data they receive from the onboard sensors.

But let's also flip the coin and consider the pilot's point of view. On the one hand, pilots still get to fly planes. And they're doing it in a much safer environment without having to be away from their family so much. It's also true that the very fact that pilots are not traveling as much could also be seen as a downside, because that means they aren't really seeing the world as part of their gig. But that may or may not be a sticking point. On the other hand, a pilot whose remote flight crashes could suffer survivor's guilt. If the pilot had been on the plane, chances are, they would have gotten injured or died just like the rest of the crew and passengers. Take that pilot off the plane, and they'll never have to suffer the immediate physical consequences and long-term effects of their actions, inactions, or mistakes, or the malfunctions of the aircraft. But they may end up paying a huge toll mentally and emotionally. Maybe they've just exchanged one occupational hazard for another. Choose your poison.

But assuming we got past the fact that the pilot wasn't onboard, and that pilots may have to deal with survivor's guilt more so than if they were actually onboard, and that humans aren't very good with multi-tasking, we'd still have to get this technology up and flying. Currently, other than remote control model airplanes, no aircraft are equipped to be flown by remote control and no airlines or airports are equipped with facilities to serve as remote control cockpits. (Military operations are the exception, but, of course, they are not going to be sharing their cockpits with commercial airliners). Building the planes is one matter. It would probably work for airliners the same as bringing any other plane through design into production and service. Building the infrastructure is another. Passenger airports were not designed with remote control cockpits in mind. Airports would need to be expanded and redesigned to some minimal extent. Then there's the construction to think about. How long will that take? How much will it cost? Where will that money come from? Will all airports come onboard? What about all airlines? How to manage the mix of remote control cockpit airports and airlines and traditional ones? Will remote control cockpit planes be restricted to certain airports?

It seems plausible that remote control cockpit planes might be restricted to certain airports in the beginning, as the technology is tested and slowly expanded. But if airlines don't see enough support and benefit building up, the investment may not be of use to them. The same goes for the airports. Nobody will want to dump millions, or maybe even billions, into infrastructure that doesn't last.

While the remote control cockpit idea is essentially keeping the same human-machine dynamic and just stretching the distance between the two participants, the attendant-pilot model requires a whole new level of automation. Without someone at the controls to more or less constantly instruct and guide the aircraft, the aircraft would be entirely responsible for the safe execution of the entire flight. That in itself is a minefield of technical issues, as discussed earlier. Of course, unlike with complete automation, in this model, the attendant-pilot would step in case of an emergency. But would that pilot be able to respond fast enough, especially if they were in the middle of serving someone their snacks? Or if *anyone* was in the middle of serving snacks? The carts would be in the way, blocking the whole aisle, and consequently that pilot's shortest path to the controls. Furthermore, it probably would do no psychological good for the passengers to see their flight attendant – and only pilot – dropping everything to scurry to the controls because of an emergency.

Considering the shortcomings of the attendant-pilot model, why not just extend this model to eliminate the human pilot altogether? That is to say, considering that the airplane's automation would have to be so majorly revamped, why not revamp it to the point that no human pilot interaction whatsoever was necessary – no attendant-pilot, no pilot in the onboard cockpit, no pilot at the remote controls? We find ourselves again at the answer of autonomous aircraft and all the issues of technological progress and commercial and social acceptance discussed earlier.

What Industry Has To Offer

Perhaps most telling for the near future of automation in aviation, however, are the current plans of key industry players. Boeing and Airbus are the two leading manufacturers of airplanes and neither of them have fully-automated – or even substantially more automated – planes in the lineup. Both companies are focusing on improving the existing technology, with careful attention paid to increasing pilots' situational awareness.[6, 8] Boeing makes a point to say that all of the changes are compatible with current ground infrastructure and that the new designs still have a "familiar look and feel",[6] hinting at maximum return for minimum investment.

Figure 3: A view inside a current Boeing cockpit, for the Boeing 747-8
"Boeing 747-8". *Boeing*. http://www.boeing.com/commercial/747/#/design-
highlights/technologically-advanced/flight-deck/deck-features/

Figure 4: Airbus's planned A380 cockpit. Notice the basic similarity to Boeing's current cockpit.
"Cockpit". *Airbus*.
http://www.airbus.com/aircraftfamilies/passengeraircraft/a380family/commonality/

Airbus takes its innovation a bit further in its "Future by Airbus" vision for "Smarter Skies" by 2050, in which it predicts the capability of swarming technology. The idea is that planes self-organize in V-formations much like birds do to maximize energy efficiency and "select the most efficient and environmentally friendly routes".[35] In the same article, Airbus reports that they are conducting studies into to the feasibility of such operations and the stability and control technology that would be required.[35] However, it seems unlikely that any such technology would be debuting anytime soon, given that they are currently in the research phase.

Figure 5: An example of Airbus's vision for swarming.
"The future: Express Skyways". *Airbus*. http://www.airbus.com/innovation/future-by-airbus/smarter-skies/aircraft-in-free-flight-and-formation-along-express-skyways/

The aviation industry is slow to change. It takes the "better part of a decade"[29] to design, build, and test-fly a conventional aircraft. The basics of cockpit automation have not changed substantially for at least thirty years. Though improvements have been made, nothing major has changed since 1972.[29] Furthermore, regulation changes must be processed through the FAA, which could also take years.

Looking Ahead...

All things considered, there seems to be no great motivation for commercial passenger aircraft to go pilotless. The technical advances required are effort and time intensive and, as of now, unlikely to render any financial benefits to the companies that undertake the challenge. The companies themselves show no inclination to tackle the technological and social complexities, not to mention the potential legislative quagmires.

On the other hand, leading aircraft producers Airbus and Boeing are improving the current technology with an eye to improved safety. It seems likely, then, that the next thirty-five years will see an improvement of the systems we already have, but not necessarily anything groundbreakingly new.

So who – or what – *will* be your pilot thirty-five years from now? What *will* our grandchildren see when they look up?

Chances are they'll see pretty much exactly what we see today, as far as commercial passenger aircraft go. When they walk into the plane, they could still – if they're lucky and the door is open – peek into the cockpit and see the familiar team of pilot and co-pilot, both human. The computer, sensor and other interfaces may be different but not substantially so. The industry players themselves may be moving towards Airbus's vision of smarter skies and flocks of planes. But beyond improved passenger safety – which may not be tangible from flight to flight but could potentially manifest itself in fewer fatal crashes in the news – the day-to-day experience of passengers will likely remain unchanged.

Make no mistake. Challenging though the path to the runway may be, autonomous aircraft could eventually take to the skies. But until that, day, our grandchildren can look forward to the familiar refrain, in the voice of a fellow human being:

"Good afternoon folks! This is your Captain speaking."

1. All Things Considered, NPR News Investigations. "Air Safety On Autopilot? Problems Spur Investigation," February 17, 2011. http://www.npr.org/2011/02/17/133814621/investigation-scrutinizes-safety-of-flight-automation.

2. "Attitude." *Dictionary.com.* Dictionary.com, LLC, 2016. http://www.dictionary.com/browse/attitude?s=t.

3. "Automatic Pilot." *Dictionary.com.* Dictionary.com, LLC, 2016. http://www.dictionary.com/browse/automatic-pilot.

4. "Autopilot." *Dictionary.com.* Dictionary.com, LLC, 2016. http://www.dictionary.com/browse/autopilot?s=t.

5. "Boeing 747-8". *Boeing.* http://www.boeing.com/commercial/747/#/design-highlights/technologically-advanced/flight-deck/deck-features/

6. "Boeing Next-Generation 737". *Boeing.* http://www.boeing.com/commercial/737ng/#/design-highlights/technologically-advanced/advanced-flight-deck/flight-deck-technologies/

7. "Can Any Aircraft Take off Using Auto-Pilot? [duplicate]." Question and Answer. *Aviation Stack Exchange*, May 2014. http://aviation.stackexchange.com/questions/3827/can-any-aircraft-take-off-using-auto-pilot.

8. "Cockpit". *Airbus.* http://www.airbus.com/aircraftfamilies/passengeraircraft/a380family/commonality/

9. Costello, Tom. "Airline Pilots Depend Too Much on Automation, Says Panel Commissioned by FAA." *NBC News*, November 19, 2013. http://www.nbcnews.com/news/other/airline-pilots-depend-too-much-automation-says-panel-commissioned-faa-f2D11625301.

10. Cox, John. "Ask the Captain: When Planes Land Themselves." *USA Today*, February 9, 2014. http://www.usatoday.com/story/travel/columnist/cox/2014/02/09/autoland-low-visibility-landings/5283931/.

11. Davies, Alex, and Aarian Marshall. "Self-Driving Cars Will Love the Driving Hell That Is Boston." *Wired: Transportation*, November 22, 2016. https://www.wired.com/2016/11/nutonomy-autonomous-cars-boston/.

12. "Difference Engine: Crash Program?" *The Economist: Babbage*, August 26, 2013. http://www.economist.com/blogs/babbage/2013/08/cockpit-automation.

13. "Flying the SE.5A". *The Vintage Aviator Ltd.* December 14, 2016. http://thevintageaviator.co.nz/projects/se-5a-reproduction/flying-se5a

14. Garrison, Peter. "Op-Ed: Germanwings Crash: No Algorithm Can Stop a Pilot Bent on Killing Himself." *Los Angeles Times.* March 26, 2015. Germanwings crash: No algorithm can stop a pilot bent on killing himself.

15. "Google Self-Driving Car Project". *Google, Inc.* https://www.google.com/selfdrivingcar/

16. Grant, R. G. *Flight: The Complete History.* (DK Publishing, 2007).

17. Greenough, John. "10 Million Self-Driving Cars Will Be on the Road by 2020." Business Insider: Tech Insider, June 15, 2016. http://www.businessinsider.com/report-10-million-self-driving-cars-will-be-on-the-road-by-2020-2015-5-6.

18. "How the Space Race Changed Computing." *PC Plus*, January 23, 2010. techradar. http://www.techradar.com/news/computing/how-the-space-race-changed-computing-665069.

19. Kedmey, Dan. "Here's Why United Flights Were Grounded This Morning." *Time: Business*, June 2, 2015. http://time.com/3904777/united-airlines-flights-grounded-glitch/.

20. Krisch, Joshua A. "What Is the Flight Management System? A Pilot Explains." *Popular Mechanics*, March 18, 2014. http://www.popularmechanics.com/flight/a10234/what-is-the-flight-management-system-a-pilot-explains-16606556/.

21. Langewiesche, William. "The Turn." *The Atlantic Monthly*, December 1993.

22. Mars, Roman (99% Invisible). "Air France Flight 447 and the Safety Paradox of Automated Cockpits." *The Eye: Slate's Design Blog*, June 25, 2015. http://www.slate.com/blogs/the_eye/2015/06/25/air_france_flight_447_and_the_safety_para dox_of_airline_automation_on_99.html.

23. Patterson, Thom. "Who's Really Flying the Plane?" *CNN Travel*, March 26, 2012. http://www.cnn.com/2012/03/24/travel/autopilot-airlines/index.html.

24. Pitas, Costas, Kylie MacLellan, and Paul (Editor) Sandle. "UK Government Announces Funding for Autonomous Vehicles, Electric Cars." *Reuters*, November 23, 2016. http://uk.mobile.reuters.com/article/idUKKBN13I1D3.

25. Purificato, Rudy. "Ocker, pioneer of 'blind flying'". *The Early Birds of Aviation, Inc.* http://www.earlyaviators.com/eocker1.htm

26. Reynolds, Quentin. *The Amazing Mr. Doolittle: A Biography of Lieutenant General James H. Doolittle*. New York: Appleton-Century-Crofts, Inc., 1953. https://archive.org/stream/amazingmrdoolitt00reyn/amazingmrdoolitt00reyn_djvu.txt.

27. Scheck, William. "Lawrence Sperry: Autopilot Inventor and Aviation Innovator." *Aviation History*. HistoryNet. Accessed December 8, 2016. http://www.historynet.com/lawrence-sperry-autopilot-inventor-and-aviation-innovator.htm.

28. Smith, Patrick. "Checked, Set, Roger." *Ask The Pilot*, September 29, 2015. http://www.askthepilot.com/checklists/.

29. Smith, Patrick. "Pilotless Planes? Not So Fast." *Ask The Pilot*, April 21, 2015. http://www.askthepilot.com/pilotless-planes/.

30. Smith, Patrick. "Q&A With The Pilot." *Ask The Pilot*, July 9, 2015. http://www.askthepilot.com/questions-2/.

31. Smith, Patrick. "Why Pilots Still Matter." *The New York Times*, April 10, 2015, sec. The Opinion Pages. http://www.nytimes.com/2015/04/10/opinion/why-pilots-still-matter.html?ref=opinion&_r=1.

32. "Sperry Sr., Lawrence Burst". *The National Aviation Hall of Fame*. http://www.nationalaviation.org/our-enshrinees/sperry-sr-lawrence-burst/

33. Stewart, Jack. "Tesla's Self-Driving Car Plan Seems Insane, But It Just Might Work." *Wired: Transportation*, October 24, 2016. https://www.wired.com/2016/10/teslas-self-driving-car-plan-seems-insane-just-might-work/.

34. Stewart, Jon. "Pilotless Passenger Planes Prepare for Take-Off." *BBC Future*, November 18, 2014. http://www.bbc.com/future/story/20130502-pilotless-planes-plan-to-take-off.

35. "The future: Express Skyways". *Airbus*. http://www.airbus.com/innovation/future-by-airbus/smarter-skies/aircraft-in-free-flight-and-formation-along-express-skyways/

36. The Tesla Team. "All Tesla Cars Being Produced Now Have Full Self-Driving Hardware." *Tesla: Blog*, October 19, 2016. https://www.tesla.com/blog/all-tesla-cars-being-produced-now-have-full-self-driving-hardware.

37. Wallace, Lane E. *Airborne Trailblazer: Two Decades With NASA Langley's 737 Flying Laboratory*. The NASA History Series. Washington, D.C.: NASA History Office, 1994. http://history.nasa.gov/SP-4216.pdf.

CHAPTER 4:

KEEPING PLANES IN THE SKY

THE FUTURE OF FUEL AND EFFICIENCY

Alexander G. Hunt – Freshman

Mechanical, Industrial and Manufacturing Engineering

Introduction

Flight is one of those magical feelings; when searching to describe an action that feels natural and serene, the first thought that comes to my mind is the sensation of flying. Ever since humans could look up and watch birds glide through the sky, we have wanted to be among them, with only the friction of the air to keep us afloat. We have now mastered powered flight, with over a century of practice. Currently, we face the prospect of losing this capability, due to the fact that our finite source of fuel has a very tangible end. This is the next major obstacle that we face in our reach for the skies. Innovation comes in the face of opposition. With war, the use of fuel injection and forced induction came into common practice. Fuel provided the upper hand to the pilots fighting for supremacy. In the face of oil crises, innovation brought winglets to reduce the drag caused by the differences in pressures above and below the wings, decreasing fuel consumption. Then there has been the challenges of what we require from aircraft, shifting materials used to construct them has been caused by the growing demands for improved flight. From wood and cloth, to aluminum, and currently to glass fiber reinforced plastics, these materials have significantly improved performance and efficiency as the needs have emerged. As problems arise, solutions come to life, born from brilliant ideas and borrowed from other fields. The solution to our current predicament is far from straightforward, and will be the culmination of work done in many areas. Very likely, the improvements will be mostly pursued in efficiency, reduction of pollution, and development of energy systems.

Efficiency

Efficiency has been the biggest driver in aviation from the beginning of human flight. Higher efficiency in engines allowed for us to take flight in the first place. As engine efficiency increased, and flights became longer, greater and bigger feats could be accomplished. From crossing the English Channel, to now flying around the world, efficiency has allowed us to conquer the sky and beyond. Now it holds potential for being one of the biggest reasons for us to be capable of staying up in the sky, as the future and all it entails comes to be.

Fuel Efficiency

So what do we face in the years to come, to allow our grandchildren to look up and see a contrail in the sky? Seeing as oil consumption is rising steadily every year at a rate of around 2.7%[i] and the certainty of no more oil reserves being made, it is obvious that even with controversial methods such as fracking, the amount of oil available will decrease at an ever growing rate. This means that soon, much sooner than what we might think, there will be no more fossil fuels to power aircraft or any other current forms of transportation that are dependent on these fuels. So how will planes stay in the sky?

This question can begin to be answered starting with efficiency. There is always the certainty of progress being made in material sciences and structural engineering. These advances have allowed for lighter and more efficient aircraft that use less fuel and travel farther, carrying more. This can be seen in the charts made from claims of efficiency by Airbus and Boeing between 1980 and 2016, which show a general and gradual trend downwards with data points to show an increase in higher efficiency. The fourth chart demonstrates a linear line of best fit from the previous three charts for greater simplicity.

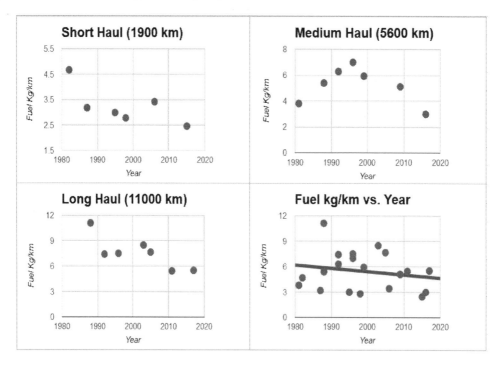

With these charts considered, a trend can be seen, and one aspect might stand out about them. For about the last 40 years, a time that makes up around a third of the 110 years we have achieved powered flight[ii], planes really haven't become that much more efficient. This is likely because, even though the price of oil has steadily risen, the price has not risen at such a rate to eliminate profit of commercial flight when counteracted by a proportional steady rise in efficiency and ticket prices. By using the trend line, shown above on the fourth chart, created by the data of approximately the last 40 years, the future can be estimated. Though not shown in the chart, the math of this approximation states that efficiency will increase by .38 kg/km every ten years, resulting in an average fuel consumption rate, for all commercial flight distances of 3.49 kg/km or a 37% increase over the current average. But there is hope for much higher efficiency, and current concept systems. Systems that have been tested and proven, specifically, blended wing bodies and propfan propulsion systems have the potential for an efficiency rise of around 50%, not including the projected rise of around 37% efficiency stated earlier. This means that by 2050 there is potential for commercial aircraft to fly with a very close or even surpass the 1 kg/km fuel mark. Similarly, fuel efficiency is climbing steadily in private aviation, but there is trouble with new aircraft costing a small fortune. It isn't feasible for most private owners to exchange their current aircraft for newer, more efficient ones. If one considers the wealth required to purchase a new aircraft, the money could instead be used to fuel and maintain the old one.

Economic Efficiency

The high cost of flight brings the conversation about economic efficiency. This could be considered through the perspective of aircraft production, but more importantly is the meaning economic efficiency when considering fuel prices. Recently the price has been driven down by new methods of mining, which means currently we are consuming more crude oil than ever. For the average American consumer, low gas prices are a welcome sight, allowing inexpensive goods and cheap travel. Still, in 2012, according to a statistics report by the International Air Transport Association, 33% of all commercial airline operating costs were fuel.[iii] But as aforementioned, our primary source of energy, crude oil, is quite finite. So what will it mean when we can no longer force it out of the earth? The effect of this will be quick: skyrocketing prices to astronomical rates, which, in our current situation, would make most flight wildly impractical. This known fact is driving research that often goes hand in hand with work to decrease and eliminate pollution. The hope is that a solution can be found in a source that isn't detrimental to the environment, or our wallets.

What a groundbreaking discovery, pertaining to the creation of new fuels, could mean for the likes of light aircraft; the price of flying would stabilize, countering the steady rise that has occurred since the first oil crises. What is important to note though is that a transition in the fuel used will also likely necessitate modifications and adaptations in order to achieve reliability and efficiency.

Transition to Simplicity

What will be important in the future is learning how to do more with less. The way that much of the world has been engineered has been in a sort of brute force manor. This means that more powerful, bigger, and stronger is better. But perhaps the way of the future is simplicity. With the average commercial and military aircraft costing in the hundreds of millions of dollars to purchase[iv], and in many instances the technology that these aircraft have at their disposal is overwhelming; it might be time to take a different look at how aircraft is manufactured. Even in private aircraft industry, most people are just simply priced out, when light aircraft cost as much as a house. Relatively, these large costs aren't due to the materials of the aircraft, which now, are making large leaps and bounds in the field of composites, but rather, these costs come from the highly technical systems that require many years to develop. As costs and complexity go up, production volume goes down, further increasing cost per airplane due to the necessity of covering overhead costs. What we are left with is highly refined aircraft that works very well, but because they were designed to function using many complex systems, it looks as though the most basic principle of aviation is ignored. This principle is simplicity, and it seems that at least when it comes to the leading edge of aircraft technology, it is only an afterthought. A comparable field to the development of modern aviation is that of computing. What has been accomplished with both is simply staggering, a feat that a few centuries ago might have been considered magic. But just like aviation, computing is meeting challenges that are forcing a change in focus. Similarly, computing has been developed using brute force, a long list of mosts and bests created by steep competition. But computing has reached a point where it can no longer continue to make big leaps in the technology, making smaller and faster, and now simpler, and arguably more important has arisen. How do they make these technologies more efficient, more reliable, and what they accomplish is smarter, in a way that is not simply through overpowering what they face. This, at the very least will have a positive effect on aviation, through direct development of technology. Potentially the development of computing effect will be more in the periphery, changing the way that engineers think.

With light aircraft, this simplicity will come in the form of computer design and small, well made, universal instrument sets that are inexpensive, easy to use, and reliable. The cost of manufacturing and development are the biggest parts of the price of production in private aircraft. Until methods are created that make this quick and easy, it is unlikely that a transition to simplicity alone will bring down the price tag of airplanes a remarkable amount, but with uses of simplicity will make aircraft more reliable and better the in world of General Aviation.

Pollution

Another challenge that we face is that of pollution, which, according to the United States Environmental Protection Agency or simply EPA, 26% of greenhouse[v] gases are created by the transportation sector. This means that if a solution for our fuel predicament is found in a source that does not produce greenhouse gases; the potential for reduction of the rate of climate change could be drastic.

Blended Fuels

A few of the currently available solutions for the pollution problem is blended alternative jet fuel, which, according to NASA, could reduce emissions up to 50%[vi]. The downfall is that, like traditional jet fuels, these fuels involve organic structures that rely on hydrocarbons to deliver energy through combustion which creates carbon dioxide, water, and other structures, that are, in most cases, greenhouse gases. Greenhouse gases affect the makeup of the atmosphere, changing the how much sunlight is absorbed into the earth's thermal system and how much is reflected back out into space. Jet fuels also contain a large amount of sulfur to provide lubrication, which when burned, creates sulfur dioxide, an ingredient of acid rain. What makes commercial airliners, private aircraft, and other forms of aviation so detrimentally effective in altering the atmosphere is their release of emissions in high altitudes, where the damage done is immediate. Add to this the long list of additives that are involved to make fuels stable, and have desirable characteristics, and the result is staggering. An example of this is made not by the existence of many flights, but rather the absence of them. In 2010 with the eruption of the Icelandic volcano Eyjafjallajökull, a plume of ash, smoke, and water vapor was shot up 30,000ft, which is the cruising height of most airline flights. This grounded many planes, making this volcano the world's first in the trend of carbon neutrality. Carbon neutrality has been a goal of many of the forward nations of the world, met by removing, sequestering, or offsetting the emissions of CO_2 created by industry, transportation, and energy generation. In the case of the eruption of the Icelandic volcano, the price we pay for transportation is comparable to continuous volcanic eruptions all over the world for as long as flights continue to be as polluting as they are.

So how do blended fuels begin to address the elephant in the room? To begin with, these fuels can involve fuel made with biomass, an example being ethanol. Ethanol has found great success in much of the world as a part in modern gasoline. Though much of the gasoline in the U.S. is less than 10% in ethanol content, elsewhere it is common to use e85, an 85% ethanol fuel, that and ethanol's non fossil fuel source, made mostly from corn, also allows for higher efficiency. This is due to its properties that lubricate, and cool the system ethanol is being used in, as well as increases boost. Therefore compression in a forced induction engine decreases fuel consumption by delivering more of the potential energy in the fuel. Similarly, other biomass sourced fuels, that have properties more similar to jet fuel, and high grade aviation fuel could be used. The trouble is, with most advanced piston engined aircraft, if they are capable of running pump gas, ethanol fuels are avoided at all costs. This is because, unless they are designed to use it, ethanol will break down the rubber seals and fuel lines, causing premature engine failure. This is easily remedied, but for most, it is, at this point, simply not worth the trouble to be fixed. With this consideration, perhaps the biggest challenge that is faced with a transition to blended fuels, or full biomass fuels is for the large majority of aircraft owners to trust in new, developed fuels which could be big risk. The change is inevitable though, and will soon follow in the footsteps of ground transportation, bringing greener fuels to the sky.

It is also Important to note, General Aviation gas is so expensive in Europe (and really everywhere else in the world other than the USA) that a rather large portion of new General Aviation aircraft is being sold with a diesel power plant option. In fact, the Cessna aircraft company offers one of their aircraft as a ready to fly diesel available for sale in the US and internationally. This is evidence of a developing market that could quickly be occupied by new types of fuels.

Non-Hydrocarbon Fuels

Another source that could potentially eliminate harmful emissions is ammonia, which due to its price point and energy density is comparable to current jet fuel. The future holds the potential to move away from carbon based fuels, into for example, nitrogen based fuels. They could theoretically work similarly, made up of a mix of compounds to get reliable and consistent, carbon-neutral jet fuels, as well as equivalents to the high octane aviation fuels. These fuels, like their hydrocarbon, biomass based cousins, can be produced through the processing of grown materials. Unlike biomass fuels though, the typical sources of nitrogen based fuels aren't byproducts of commercially grown food staples, but rather come from far more common and abundant nitrogen fixing Cyanobacteria. Incorrectly known as blue green algae, they are only loosely related to true algae, and are far simpler in structure. Typically as part of their relationship with plants these "algae" can produce ammonia, nitrites, and nitrates, products that may lead us into a carbon neutral future. The reason why they, if these fuels are chosen for the future, have the potential to have such a small impact, is that when burned, the only greenhouse gas they produce is water, and the nitrogen becomes nitrogen gas, the most abundant gas in our planet's atmosphere. These fuels can be used in both jet engines and in internal combustion engines, but currently there are a few problems. As a jet fuel, its energy density is around half that of current conventional kerosene, which would eliminate, without a big jump in efficiency, its use in transcontinental, and transoceanic flights, because commercial airliners just couldn't hold enough fuel. But if it was implemented today, it could be used in medium to short range flights, and would prove to be a cost effective and environmentally friendly solution. Another problem is, that, and this affects light, private aircraft more, is that it requires a well sealed tank, and can be very dangerous if a living organism is exposed to it, due to its reactivity. With proper precaution though, it too could be implemented as a replacement for aviation fuel, through it would require development of the engines that it would be burned in.

Policy

Pollution created by fleets of aircraft could be reduced more simply through new policies. First on the list is the need for taxiing more efficiently. In 2010 passengers spent the time equivalent of 91 years on the runway, burning an unnecessary 200 million gallons of fuel[vii]. This waste could be minimized through lowering the amount of time spent getting to and from the runway, as well as the time spent on the runway, through keeping airplanes at the gate until they can continue to flight quickly. Further gains could be made through using a single engine in taxiing, or even further by using an electric wheel in the landing gear, cutting 2.8 percent of carbon emissions, on average, per flight.

Next is ensuring that excess weight is cut. This can be done, firstly, through ensuring that the contingency fuel that is stored to be burned during an emergency in flight, is only as much needed in case of an emergency. A study done at George Washington University estimated that a 661 pound reduction in contingency fuel would save an average of 11,000 gallons of fuel[viii]. In addition to this, further reduction requires lighter parts, better designed interiors, and as much lightweight materials as possible. It is important to note, that the lighter aircraft are, the less fuel they need to burn, and therefore the less pollution they make.

Another act that would have a positive effect on the efficiency of a fleet would be the required retirement or refurbishment of airliners after a set number of years. This would allow for the use of new technologies to come to main stage, as well as ensure that tired old jet engines aren't wasting fuel unnecessarily.

In privately owned aircraft, the policy that will help fleets, will not have a largely noticeable effect, but could benefit in other ways, rather than a decrease in pollution. For instance, better automation in the way of traffic control would allow for busier airports, with less time spent wasted taxiing, or in forms of non-essential flight.

Energy Systems

Efficiency is also taking leaps and bounds with sources of energy not fully reliant upon internal combustion or turbine power. A few of these technologies can be seen in the Helios Prototype. On this NASA prototype, a fully solar powered UAV, is included the storage of extra energy with electrolysis to later be used by a hydrogen fuel cell[ix]. In addition to this, leaps and bounds have been made in test bed and concept aircraft using hybrid systems. Though these systems are far from practical, the future has much in store. A pattern for this can be seen in the past. Forced induction, that was born to give life to early diesel engines used on ground vehicles quickly developed to be practical for high altitude internal combustion engines by giving them the air necessary to counteract low atmospheric density. This happened over the course of a few decades.

Fuel Cells

Looking back at NASA's Helios Prototype there is potential for a battery system that is far less detrimental than other metal based ones. Using hydrogen fuel cells in combination with electrolysis has tempting potential when considered as a battery substitute. The theory behind this is, that to store energy, water is separated into diatomic hydrogen and oxygen, in which there can be a loss of energy in heat, but then the energy is used through a reverse chemical reaction that can, with the capture of heat, end up at around 85% efficiency. An upside of this method of energy storage is that it doesn't lose storage capacity, has a high energy density, and does not, in any stage of production, require substances harmful to the environment. Downsides are that it is not as straightforward as a traditional battery, and there is much higher loss of energy if the energy produced by the fuel cell is allowed to be lost through heat. These systems could make their way into commercial airliners, but first they will have to make leaps and bounds in experimental aircraft. Another trouble is that, as battery technology makes leaps and bounds, closing the gap, it may end up that fuel cells never have the chance to make it off the ground on a large scale. But if they do, this technology shows promise for ultra light aircraft, similar to the Helios.

Hybrid Systems

Likewise, hybrid systems have been developing and becoming commonplace in ground transportation, with nearly every major automotive company developing their own line. Though in aviation it is nowhere near as straightforward, commercial airliners could be developed to slightly offset their dependence on jet fuel by using solar arrays and electric motors to increase efficiency in a visible way. Another possibility is the idea of electric jets, which could take form as ducted fans. This, with current battery technology, isn't viable, but could become viable by using hyper efficient piston engines paired with turbochargers designed to run at their most efficient speed, thereby eliminating some of the efficiency problems caused by gas turbines. The problem with Hybrid energy systems is that there is far more trust in conventional turbine engines, and if Hybrids are to succeed they must first work on a smaller scale. The good thing is that this technology has the potential to be much more straightforward in non-turbine aircraft. A hybrid system could lower the power needed from a piston engine, such that it can be optimized for cruising with the assistance of the electric motor for takeoff and maneuvers. In addition to this an electric motor greatly increases the safety of light aircraft, eliminating the loss of all power if the main engine fails, giving more time to make a safe emergency landing. Similar to the systems of the Helios aircraft, a hybrid aircraft could benefit from solar panels, which, theoretically, could develop the aircraft into planes that need little to no power from piston engines.

Propfans

Another system that shows promise is that of propfans, which are, as defined by the European Aviation Safety Agency, "a turbine engine featuring contra rotating fan stages not enclosed within a casing." Essentially this propulsion system takes the best of a turboprop and a turbofan, making a high speed, high efficiency engine, which, although may be limited to speeds at around 450 mph, has been tested to be 30% more efficient than conventional turbofans. This is a big improvement, and it is highly likely that, with some development of the technology, these will become dominant in the market for short range flights. Developed in the 1980s to combat rising fuel prices, interest in propfans fell as fuel prices came back down. The trouble with their development was that, like all propulsion systems, they need years of refinement, because without these years propfans are lacking in performance and were louder than a conventional turboprop. Now though, as fuel prices are continuing their steady climb, propfans have peaked interest again, and have seen research funding by many aviation corporations. The reason why propfans are so efficient is because of the high bypass ratio that they are able to achieve. This essentially means that due to the external fan blade design, they are able to move large amounts of air on the outside, while requiring less air, and therefore less fuel in the body of the turbine, allowing for lower fuel consumption. Propfans benefit from contra-rotating scimitar shaped fan blades, designed to limit the shockwaves caused by spinning at supersonic speeds, and therefore decrease drag and unwanted noise. Below is a diagram that illustrates the propfan's unique characteristics, t could be said that it is quite a visually appealing engine.

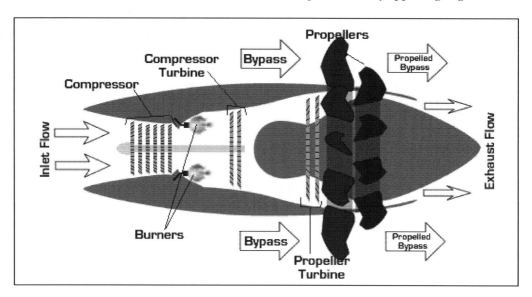

On a smaller scale, the propfan is also an appealing engine for light aircraft due to its high efficiency and thrust. Though it will likely be far out of the price range of the average enthusiast, as most jet engines are, the technology of propfans could make private jets far more friendly to the environment.

Nuclear Power

Will there even be contrails to see when our grandchildren look up? Perhaps not. To go into the future we must look into the past. As part of the Cold War, Nuclear powered aircraft were developed as long range bombers for the U.S. and the Soviets. However, the nuclear power technology of these aircraft was limited by the aircraft's crew., Due to the inability to create sufficient shielding to protect the crew from radiation poisoning, the nuclear power systems onboard these aircraft were never used. Consequently, these human health drawbacks limited the use of nuclear power in any passenger air carrier application. Another massive downfall is the idea that nuclear power is too dangerous to be used at all. So this is where material science comes in. In the past few decades, leaps and bounds have been made in the field of composites, which allow products to be lighter and stronger. Research in material science can only continue to grow, which means potentially the solution for radiation shielding is just around the corner, such as a new ceramic or alloy that allows for complete diffusion of dangerous particles. A material like this would mean a complete re-evaluation of nuclear power, and if feasible, our future of flight could be powered by the atom.

In light aircraft (and eventually Personal Air Vehicles), nuclear power holds potential to put everyone in the sky, with its massively high energy density and, in the case of fusion, easily obtainable fuels. The trouble is that even if the technology was there in 30 years, the stigma will not have gone away. We simply don't trust it enough, as it is the weapon of mass destruction, and it is difficult to look past its beginnings.

The Future of Fuel and Efficiency

The future has potential for many things as the world works to keep planes in the sky. The skies may be bluer and the stars may be clearer. As the past has shown, hopeful systems will rise and fall with only a few being good enough to be a part of the solution. So what can be predicted about the future of aviation? A rise in efficiency is inevitable, and in the next 30 years, can be in the range of only 25% on average to something near 75% if current developing technologies deliver what has been promised. In terms of economic efficiency, it is highly likely that prices of fuel and aircraft will continue on their current path, and even if drivers change, it is hard to get away from the trend of bigger, better, faster. Blended fuels will come as well, and aircraft are soon to follow in the footsteps of ground transportation. Non-hydrocarbon fuels have hope, but seeing as it is much harder to cut cold turkey than it is to gradually make the transition away from something, at least when it comes to industry. So unless a blended fuel with ammonia is devised, or, the fuel is blended in the combustion chamber, the likelihood of nitrogen based fuel taking main stage is slim. New policy has the potential to cut down on waste, and it is likely that in the years to come, the simplest answer for fleets will be the right one. Similarly, Hydrogen Fuel cells are competing with battery technology. They have potential to be a superior system, but because there is a commitment to traditional batteries, the likelihood of them ever seeing the light of day in the future systems of aviation is low. More promising though are hybrid systems, which, alongside blended fuels, will become a part of aviation in the future. Propfans show promise for the future, and hopefully they will become common in aviation, driven by increased fuel costs. The longest shot though, is the prospect of nuclear fuels, due to their unpopularity and impracticality.

[i] https://en.wikipedia.org/wiki/Oil_depletion

[ii] https://airandspace.si.edu/exhibitions/wright-brothers/online/fly/index.cfm

[iii] http://www.iata.org/pressroom/pr/Pages/2013-07-16-01.aspx

[iv] http://www.wsj.com/articles/SB10001424052702303649504577494862829051078

[v] https://www.epa.gov/ghgemissions/sources-greenhouse-gas-emissions#transportation

[vi] http://www.nasa.gov/aero/nasa-reports-alternative-jet-fuel-research-results.html

[vii] http://www.pbs.org/newshour/rundown/these-7-simple-airplane-fixes-could-halve-carbon-emissions-at-little-to-no-cost/

[viii] http://gradworks.umi.com/33/44/3344914.html

[ix] http://www.nasa.gov/centers/dryden/news/NewsReleases/2002/02-24_pf.html

[x] https://upload.wikimedia.org/wikipedia/commons/a/ab/NB-36H_with_B-50%2C_1955_-_DF-SC-83-09332.jpeg

CHAPTER 5:

GOING ANEW

THE FUTURE OF AIR TRANSPORT

Zohar Hoter, Sophomore

Mechanical, Industrial and Manufacturing Engineering

Introduction

Although originally developed to explain changes in animal species over time, the theory of evolution also applies to developments in aircraft. As newer, more beneficial traits such as lighter weight materials and monoplanes with swept wings emerged; they overtook and replaced their older counterparts. However, evolution in commercial air travel has gone stale, and aircraft have remained only slightly modified for many decades. As the metal birds of the sky become poised for speciation, a new way of commercial air travel is on the horizon.

History of Commercial Aviation

There are several important differences between the aircraft from the dawn of commuter travel and those of today. First, the piston engines of the DC3, built in the 1930's, were replaced by the entirely new jet engines of the 1950's, and even those are a far cry from today's high bypass turbofans. Second, a pilot used to the glass screens and automation of the computer age would also find himself lost among the "round dial" instrumentation of an older flight deck. Third, while the gleam of a DC3 would result from its silvery unpainted skin, the Boeing 787's composite would not shine at all if left unpainted. Finally, the wings of older airliners had little to no sweep and been adorned with fuel tanks, whereas newer airliners have sleek and highly refined wings with graceful lines, ornamented by winglets and sharklets to decrease drag.

Despite this, from a distance, an Airbus and Boeing of today would be almost indistinguishable from one of 1980. The configuration of a long cigar-shaped body, two wings and a tail has persevered since the DC3. There are several reasons for this norm, such as materials, simplicity, and tradition. However, as these reasons dissipate with advancing technologies, a new era of airliners could dawn.

Boeing 737-130 on landing is almost indistinguishable from a more recent airliner- The Museum of Flight

Looking Forward

There will be several indicators of change to come. Firstly, flying prototypes will be developed to prove new technologies that have been vetted in scaled and computer modeling. Many proposals exist and several of them are radically different, but as of yet, they all exist as models in wind tunnels or unmanned drones. In preparation for these flying prototypes to enter service, new regulations will have to be adopted regarding airworthiness and safety. Lobbies will bring these concerns to regulatory agencies as new designs mature and become ready for service. Finally, the first adopters of any radically new technologies will be the military rather than civilian markets. The appearance of new cargo aircraft, which are often close cousins of civilian aircraft, will be a good indicator that we will soon fly aboard on a new species of metal birds.

The primary drivers for commercial aircraft in the future are going cleaner and faster. Pursuant to these demands, aircraft design will likely diverge in the near future, and reconverge as the desired traits are integrated into each other. This chapter will discuss the physics behind high speed and low speed flight, the history of two very different kinds of flight, and how airliners in the next 50 years will become two very different species- one blisteringly fast and one an economic workhorse.

Going Faster

As World War Two ended, supersonic flight was considered impossible. Pilots who approached the sound barrier during dives experienced buffeting and vibration forces that proved irreversible for many. As their aircraft were pushed to the limit, pilots of World War Two began to speak of the speed of sound as an impenetrable wall beyond which controlled flight was impossible[i]. What was it that these pilots were encountering?

The Sonic Boom

Before we go any further, we need to understand the speed of sound and supersonic flight. Sound is made up of pressure waves around us that are translated into vibrations and then signals that the human brain interprets. The speed of sound is the speed at which these waves can move through air. This is also a measure of how quickly compressed air can decompress. It is a property of the gas that changes with the humidity, temperature, and altitude. At sea level, in dry air, at 68 degrees Fahrenheit, the speed of sound is 768 miles per hour.

Now, imagine a boat. As it travels faster, it begins creating a wake that trails behind it and eventually dissipates. This wake is made up of water that cannot move out of the way of the boat fast enough, and is actually compressed into a higher pressure region. If the boat travels fast enough, the wake even forms in front of it. If the boat travels even faster, it rides up on this bow wave. A similar phenomenon occurs in aircraft. As the aircraft moves through the air, it creates a wake of turbulent air and higher pressure air around it. As it travels faster, it compresses air in front of it. This is, in effect, a shockwave. The faster the aircraft flies the more compressed and energetic it's shockwave. A sonic boom is a shock wave created from supersonic flight[ii].

An F/A 18 accelerating through the sound barrier with a vapor cloud revealing the shockwave around it- NASA

As our hypothetical airplane approaches that speed, it catches up to the pressure wave in front of it. Between mach 0.8 and 1.0, also called the transonic region, the range of speeds of the airflows around the airplane are concurrently below, at, and above the speed of sound. This means that the airplane is now in its own shockwave.

Flight in the transonic region is known for being especially violent if an aircraft is not engineered properly. The uneven and extreme compressions on the different surfaces of the aircraft can cause harsh vibrations and the high pressure on control surfaces can cause them to lock up. This is what caused the demise of those many aforementioned WWII pilots, and gave reason for others to declare the speed of sound as an insurmountable obstacle.

A mere two years later, they would be proven wrong as the Bell X-1 broke the sound barrier for the first time[iii]. By the late 1960's, fighter jets like the F-4 Phantom broke the sound barrier on a routine basis and the SR-71 Blackbird, unknown to the public, cruised at three times the speed of sound on the edge of space.

History of Supersonic Flight in the Commercial Era

In 1969, the BAC Concorde and Tupolev TU-144 became the first commercial transports to go supersonic. The Concorde entered service in 1976 and began flying regular transatlantic routes. Although enjoying a relatively long service until 2003, the Concorde was not without its faults. At its introduction, flights to the United States were not granted permission due to citizen protest over the sonic boom that the aircraft would create. This was also the case in India and Malaysia. A few months later, routes were opened between Europe and Dulles Regional Airport[iv]. Throughout the aircraft's career, overland flights would prove to be a challenge and routing often included a deceleration or aversion of landmasses, particularly on flights to Mexico City which had to pass over Florida.

Fuel consumption would also prove to be a challenge for the Concorde. Turbofans, with their large frontal areas, created too much drag to cruise at supersonic speeds. Accordingly, four Olympus 593 afterburning turbojets, originally designed for a nuclear strike bomber, were selected to power the Concorde. Consequently, fuel consumption and pollution were high.

Of over 100 orders for the aircraft made around the time of its first flight, all but 14 were cancelled[v]. The Concorde was eventually retired from service by both British Airways and Air France in 2003. Having never made a profit, and with the manufacturer ending support for maintenance, the only commercial supersonic aircraft in service was laid to rest[vi].

While the obstacles that the Concorde faced still exist, interest in a supersonic transport has not waned. Many concepts exist to solve each of the respective flaws in the design, but very few have gained traction. In accordance with NASA goals regarding noise and environmental impact, Lockheed Martin accepted a contract in partnership with Stanford University and General Electric to generate a supersonic concept. The result of this study is the most advanced concept in the area, and it forms the basis for a manned "X-Plane" technology demonstrator. Named LM-1044 or QueSST (Quiet Super-Sonic Transport), it is the most likely outcome for the future.

The QueSST- What Will It Be?

The most important thing for any supersonic transport is that it be quiet, and the shape of the QueSST will reflect that. Current FAA regulations ban over land flights that create a sonic boom. The most recent policy statement on the matter from 2008 states: "any future supersonic airplane produce no greater noise impact on a community than a subsonic airplane"[vii].

While many approaches have been proposed for achieving this noise reduction, the one that is utilized by QueSST is to simply make the nose of the aircraft longer. Unfortunately, lengthening the nose by too much could cause problems during taxi or with fitting into the aircraft gate. Regardless, it is likely that whatever our grandkids see when they look up will have a much more pointed appearance. This long nose could also hinder forward visibility, requiring forms of synthetic vision, as well as increased automation in the cockpit[viii].

The wings of the aircraft will be radically different. As on the Concorde, a Delta wing or other highly swept shape will likely be utilized, further adding to the pointedness of the aircraft. Various contours are also likely to be added, especially around the engine inlets and other protruding features, in order to keep pressure waves formed ahead of these features from merging with each other. The result of all this on the ground is expected to be a low rumbling, rather than a single loud, and potentially damaging, thunderclap.

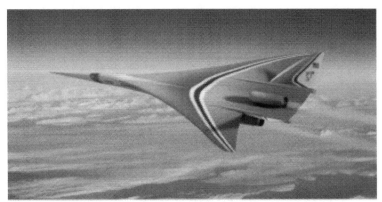

The LM1044 concept being studied by NASA and Lockheed
Skunkworks- NASA

The aircraft will also be much smaller. While single aisle jets of today (B737 A320) can seat up to 200 passengers[ix], the first QueSSTs are likely to be much smaller vehicles, carrying slightly fewer than 100 passengers. Despite this, the aircraft will likely weigh more due to the necessary fuel and materials to achieve and sustain supersonic flight. The QueSST will also have a similar range to single aisle airliners of today.

There are many human factors to consider in supersonic transport. When the Concorde flew, air compression and skin drag caused the whole skin of the aircraft to heat up, and the windows were hot to the touch. Climate control would have to adequately counter this effect. Further, the composites that this aircraft would likely be made of would have to withstand this heat, a challenge for many modern composites. Flight on board a QueSST could also be much louder than conventional aircraft, and aero acoustic considerations must be made. Finally, the proposed mission profile for supersonic transport includes several climbs, as well as accelerations and decelerations. These could be harsh on passengers or restrict them to their seats for a longer time than they are used to, and considerations may be made to minimize any discomfort caused by the handling of the aircraft, especially through the notorious transonic range[x].

The "X-plane" demonstrator to prove the technology of the QueSST has been coined LM606. With its engines already being ground tested, it is hoped that it could make its first flight by 2019[xi].

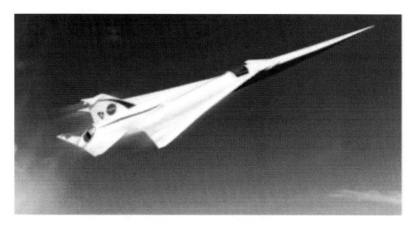

An artist's rendering of the LM606 X-plane- NASA

Going Better

On November 4th, 2016, the "Paris Agreement" entered force as nearly 200 countries agreed to keep global temperature rise to two degrees above pre-industrial levels[xii]. As the environmental impact of modern lifestyles becomes more and more destructive, reducing emissions and increasing efficiency become paramount. Efficiency and environmental impact are, and will continue to be, primary concerns in aircraft design and driving forces behind any changes in the way we fly.

Principals of Flight

An aircraft flies by propelling itself through the air using thrust and moving air over the wings. The wing is shaped in an airfoil which, by virtue of its curved upper surface, 'bends' the airflow and redirects it downwards. According to Newton's third law, for every action there must be an equal and opposite reaction. As the redirected air is the action, its reaction is an upwards force on the wing, called lift, which counteracts gravity. It is primarily this lift that allows aircraft to fly.

Unfortunately, this lift comes at a price. Since some of the airflows horizontal velocity has now been redirected downwards, there must also be a reaction to account for that in the form of a slowing, or drag, force on the wing. This is also known as induced drag. It is not to be confused with parasitic drag which occurs as a result of jutting objects from the surface of the aircraft, as well as skin drag which is friction created by the airflow over the surface of the aircraft. All surfaces, including the wing, create parasitic drag. Because drag resists forward movement through the air, engines have to produce more thrust to overcome it.

Understanding these principles of flight is key to making aircraft more efficient. The goal is to maximize lift while minimizing drag. By making wings long and skinny, there is more span creating lift at the same cost of drag. Further, by minimizing jutting surfaces and unnatural angles parasitic drag can be reduced. The area where the wing connects to the main fuselage of a cigar-shaped aircraft generates high amounts of drag. By blending this area of the wing into the body, the high drag zone can be eliminated. Finally, the Fuselage of the aircraft is a large surface area that creates drag, but does not contribute any lift. If the wings are blended even further into the body then more lift can be created and the lift to drag ratio is made more favorable.

It is from these conclusions that the concept of the Blended Wing Body and Flying Wing emerge. Championed by Boeing in conjunction with NASA, the blended wing body has no distinct fuselage and is a radical departure from the norm. By forming an aerofoil about the entire width of the aircraft, and therefore utilizing the fuselage's area aerodynamically, the aircraft skin drag can be reduced and lift can be increased[xiii].

History of the Flying Wing and Blended Body

The flying wing and blended body are not new concepts. Throughout World War Two many flying wing concepts were built and flown by both sides. One of the more notable was the Northrop Grumman YB-35, which took its first flight in 1946. This aircraft suffered from many drawbacks, mostly related to its reciprocating engines. After it was fitted with jet engines and renamed the YB-49, it again proved the benefits of the flying wing design. Unfortunately, it was too little too late as the project was behind schedule and over budget, and the YB-49 was scrapped. The legacy of the YB-49 is carried in the B-2 spirit bomber, also made by Northrop Grumman[xiv].

The B-2 Spirit is one of the only existing BWB's - Northrop Grumman

The Blended Wing Body- What Will It Be?

As interest grows in the commercial area for blended wing aircraft, research has been conducted. The X48 unmanned aircraft is a technology demonstrator built by Boeing and NASA. Taking its first flight in 1997, the program was subsequently cancelled and then reopened. The X48 is currently on its third iteration, the X48C, and plans for a manned demonstrator are underway[xv].

As with any revolutionary design, the BWB will face challenges in adoption. Previous interest in flying wings for commercial purposes was hindered by apprehension at the wide, theatre type seating it would require. This was also considered one of the primary safety issues, as there would be fewer doors placed in unconventional locations which could slow evacuation. Furthermore, in order to realize the full potential aerodynamic benefits of the design, the engines would have to be placed on top and behind the cabin. There are fears that in the event of a crash, they could dislodge and fall onto the passengers. Fitting a blended wing aircraft into a gate, or matching a boarding sleeve to it could also be a challenge, and taxiways might have to be widened to accommodate the new aircrafts girth. All of these considerations will have to be taken into account before the blended body is adopted.

Despite these drawbacks, the benefits of the blended wing are overwhelming. According to industry studies, the blended wing could use twenty percent less fuel flying at high cruise speeds in the subsonic range. It would also have a seven thousand nautical mile range, rivaling that of a Boeing 787 and putting most airport pairs within reach. The composite construction would make the aircraft weigh less, and the high efficiency engines would make less noise and produce fewer emissions[xvi].

A BWB model in wind tunnel testing - Boeing

Conclusion- Our Grandchildren and Beyond

Our grandchildren will inherit from us a new sky. When they look up, the gleaming metal birds that they see will not be ones we see. While some may be recognizable, and some may be of the new species, it is possible that they will witness the birth of an even newer aircraft. The power necessary to propel an aircraft supersonically is not yet possible with environmentally friendly turbofans, and the flying wing is not yet suitable for supersonic flight. However, as the respective technologies mature, these limitations will fade and a supersonic, environmental and economic, flying Blended Wing Body will emerge.

It has been said that the timeline of human history is strung on exploration, and how we get there. From the moment man left the cave, going somewhere has always been the goal. As we go, we leave behind a trail of innovation and development. Commercial aircraft find themselves at the intersection of many trails. From composites and autonomy, to aerodynamics and power plants, the silver gleaming birds of the sky are about to undergo a new evolution.

[i] "Faster Than Sound" PBS. October 14, 1997. Accessed December 10, 2016.
http://www.pbs.org/wgbh/nova/transcripts/2412barrier.html.

[ii] Dunbar, Brian. NASA. Accessed October 21, 2016. https://www.nasa.gov/audience/forstudents/k-4/stories/nasa-knows/what-is-supersonic-flight-k4.html.

[iii] "Faster Than Sound" PBS. October 14, 1997. Accessed December 10, 2016.
http://www.pbs.org/wgbh/nova/transcripts/2412barrier.html.

[iv] Donin, Robert B. "Safety Regulation of the Concorde Supersonic Transport: Realistic Confinement of the National Environmental Policy Act." *Hein Online*.
http://heinonline.org/HOL/LandingPage?collection=journals&handle=hein.journals/tportl8&div=7&id=&page=.

[v] Avrane, Alexandre. "CONCORDE SST :ORDERS." CONCORDE SST :ORDERS. 2013. Accessed October 20, 2016. http://www.concordesst.com/history/orders.html.

[vi] Avrane, Alexandre. "Early Development." CONCORDE SST : EARLY HISTORY - EARLY DEVELOPMENT. 2013. Accessed October 20, 2016.
http://www.concordesst.com/history/eh2.html.

[vii] Department of Transportation. Federal Aviation Administration. *Civil Supersonic Airplane Noise Type Certification Standards and Operating Rules*.

[viii] Bennett, Jay. "How NASA Wants To Build a Supersonic Plane Without the Boom." Popular Mechanics. June 13, 2016. Accessed October 21, 2016.
http://www.popularmechanics.com/flight/a21312/nasas-low-boom-supersonic-aircraft/.

[ix] 737 Airplane Characteristics for Airport Planning. PDF. Boeing, September 2013.

[x] "Advanced Concept Studies for Supersonic Commercial Transports Entering Service in the 2018-2020 Period Phase 2." NTRS, August 13, 2015. Accessed October 2016.

[xi] Bennett, Jay. "NASA Is Testing the Engine For Its Quiet-Boom Supersonic Jet." Popular Mechanics. August 11, 2016. Accessed October 21, 2016.
http://www.popularmechanics.com/flight/a22279/nasa-quiet-boom-supersonic-jet-engine/.

[xii] "Paris Climate Deal Enters Force as Focus Shifts to Action." BBC News. November 04, 2016. Accessed December 11, 2016. http://www.bbc.com/news/science-environment-37872111.

[xiii] Pilot's Handbook of Aeronautical Knowledge, 2009. Oklahoma City, OK: United States Department of Transportaton, Federal Aviation Administration, 2009.

[xiv] Dunbar, Brian. "Blended Wing Body – A Potential New Aircraft Design." NASA. April 22, 2008. Accessed October 21, 2016. https://www.nasa.gov/centers/langley/news/factsheets/FS-2003-11-81-LaRC.html.

[xv] "Boeing's X-48C Completes Flight Tests." UPI. April 12, 2013. Accessed October 21, 2016.
http://www.upi.com/Business_News/Security-Industry/2013/04/12/Boeings-X-48C-completes-flight-tests/UPI-84741365783426/.

[xvi] Dunbar, Brian. "Blended Wing Body – A Potential New Aircraft Design." NASA. April 22, 2008. Accessed October 21, 2016. https://www.nasa.gov/centers/langley/news/factsheets/FS-2003-11-81-LaRC.html.

CHAPTER 6:

WORKER BEES OF THE INFORMATION AGE

THE FUTURE OF DRONES

Mitchell F. Bernards, Junior

Mechanical, Industrial and Manufacturing Engineering

Introduction to drones

The word "drone" was projected into popularity at the end of 2013. Amazon, a global book vendor and distributor of a vast array of goods announced that it was looking to use drones in the future as a way of delivering packages. This new technology promised fast delivery times, sometimes less than 30 minutes after the order was placed. This announcement, right before the holiday season, garnered the attention of many people and brought up questions about the roles that drones will play in society

In the coming decades the technology behind drones will rapidly evolve, and they will become commonplace in society. Once drones overcome the initial learning curve they will take on many roles in society, streamlining our lives, and serving as the human to computer interface in an increasingly computer governed world.

The term "drone" has been used to describe many products that are being marketed to consumers such as "Camera drones"; a common remote controlled quadcopter with a camera attatched. However, this use of the word drone does not hold true to its definition; "An unmanned aircraft or ship that can navigate autonomously"[i]. Most of what is referenced as "drones" are not drones, but instead remote controlled aircraft.

Drones will come in many different shapes and forms; ranging from helicopters to airplanes. A VTOL is a type of aircraft that can take off and land like a helicopter and can fly like an airplane while in transit. The VTOL configuration will be ideal for many circumstances, allowing for takeoff, landing, and maneuvering in tight spaces with an efficient form of forward flight to cover long distances. Another common design is the multirotor platform, a mechanically simpler design that functions similarly to a helicopter. Multirotor designs (most notable quadcopters) make use of multiple fixed pitch propellers to generate the lift needed. Pitch, yaw, and roll are accomplished by speeding up and slowing down different rotors in contrast to a traditional helicopter that varies the pitch of its blades for different parts of a rotation which moves the center of lift away from the center of mass, which causes a change in direction. The quadcopter designs require less design effort to perfect and are arguably safer to fly close to people.

Military Drones

Many innovations are driven by defense research. The GPS system and the Internet are examples of projects that were developed with funding by the U.S. military. The U.S. has a growing interest in unmanned aerial vehicles. Removing the human element from aircraft will increase their effectiveness and limit the loss of life in future conflicts.

The flagship project that is underway is Northrop Grumman's X-47b, a flying wing that is fully computer controlled. Tests spanning from 2012 to 2014 saw the aircraft perform maneuvers from mid air refueling to taking off and landing on an aircraft carrier[ii]. These tests represent very challenging situations for traditional pilots. Another one of the tests involved the X-47b taking off from an aircraft carrier in formation with a manned fighter jet. These demonstrations show the trust that is being placed in completely autonomous drones, and how the flight controllers are able to carry out precision tasks.

Northrop Grumman X-47b

Military research is necessary to advance certain technologies quickly. Both the internet and GPS were designed to be military technologies, and in the end were adapted for civilian use. The experiments that the military is conducting with the X-47B are beyond the scope of what the FAA allows smaller drone companies to pursue. Having the X-47b taking off along manned aircraft is one example that the FAA will take notice of, showing them the accuracy and reliability of fully autonomous drones. In the end these flight controller technologies will work their way into nonmilitary applications where our grandchildren will interact with them as part of society. The remainder of this chapter will explore the nonmilitary applications of these drones and their barriers.

Why drones are ideal

There are many circumstances where drones are a better tool to use than land vehicles. Among computer controlled vehicles there are land, air and sea vehicles. There is much more flexibility for air vehicles to integrate with the way cities are built. Major cities such as Manhattan are built very densely and experience traffic issues. In these cities there is no easy way to expand the road network, and self driving cars will make these streets worse.

One issue with land vehicles is navigation. With current road networks land vehicles have very fine tolerances for their position while driving. These vehicles also have to avoid and maneuver around pedestrians, who could be considered even less predictable than car traffic. Many of the issues with self driving vehicles arise from their close proximity to humans and other cars. Aircraft, on the other hand can keep a further distance from obstacles while they are in transit, thereby creating larger margins for positioning error.

Aerial vehicles also have an easier time navigating from point A to B. Once aircraft have cleared the ground they have freedom to travel in a straight line to their destinations. This freedom of flight allows drones to take direct routes, which can save time from following road networks. These increases in air traffic raise valid concerns about how manned aircraft and drones will interact. The FAA is the main organization responsible for mandating how the two types of aircraft will respect each other's airspace. Over the past decade they have been slow to implement changes in their laws as aircraft technology has advanced fairly slowly. In order for the drone industry to flourish the FAA needs to significantly rewrite their aircraft regulations or speed up the updating process for laws.

A thought experiment can show the differences between how cars and aerial vehicles navigate. If 1,000 drones and 1,000 cars were to leave the Portland metro area and travel to Seattle Washington the cars would make their way to i-5 and travel along one common road until they got to Seattle, at which point they could spread out to their destinations. Meanwhile, the drones are not limited to funnel through a narrow space and can spread out to reduce interference. Because the drones can spread out over larger areas they can keep a larger distance between each other. This benefits the drones in several ways. Because they are spread far apart they will spend a much smaller portion of their flight time actively avoiding other aircraft than self driving cars spend avoiding other cars. This allows the drones to spend a much greater amount of time operating as efficiently as possible towards their goal; delivering packages faster and extending their range through more efficient flight.

Electronic Advancements

A separate part of the drone design process includes specifying the control system, which requires advanced computer processors and sensors to gather the data needed to accomplish the assigned mission. Computers are a rapidly evolving technology. The computers that controlled the Saturn 5 rocket weighed 72.5 pounds and could perform 12,000 calculations per second. The computer that was used in the rocket performed very rudimentary flight controls. A course was pre- programmed ahead of time. During flight the computer tried to keep the rocket as close to the initial path as possible based off accelerometer data. While, at the time the programming was considered highly complex similar systems are now taught to kids through robotics introduction kits in the form of line following cars.

Modern micro controllers the size of a dime can process 12 billion calculations per second while consuming less than ¼ the electrical power required for the Saturn 5's computer[iii]. This increase in processing power allows for advanced control systems to be implemented.

As of 2015 some of the cutting edge research in computer control systems involves what is called "neural networks". Rather than telling a computer a very specific set of constraints in order to get a desired outcome the computer is given large amounts of data of correct results and incorrect results. The computer is then left to determine what is an ideal outcome. One example of where this could be used is for package delivery drones to determine landing zones. It would be nearly impossible for programmers to quantify the correlations between vision and LIDAR scans to determine where to land. Trying to solve this problem using deep learning would involve showing the computer images and laser scans of ideal and non-ideal landing zones. The computer would use pattern recognition to determine what all of the ideal landing zones have in common, and would then look for these traits once in control of a drone. This form of programming opens up possibilities to solve many problems, at the cost of higher processing requirements. Full utilization of deep learning will occur as computers progress in their capabilities.

Aside from the benefits of having more processing power to run the flight control software the miniaturization of computers also benefits flight time. Aircraft will consume more power if they weigh more regardless of whether they are a helicopter or an airplane. Lightweight computer hardware will keep the aircraft efficient while in flight. Another benefit comes from the reduction in electricity consumption. This is especially important for smaller drones that rely on electrical propulsion. Energy efficient computers will leave more power in the battery for flight.

There is a proposed mathematical equation that predicts the advancement of computer hardware over time. Gordon Moore, the cofounder of Fairchild semiconductor and Intel published a paper in 1965 predicting that the number of transistors in a computer chip would double every two years[iv]. Semiconductors are small switches that will respond to the actions of others. In very large networks these switches can perform the mathematical operations that power computers. As the transistor networks get larger more complex operations can be performed, and many operations can be processed at the same time. This is one of the driving factors behind the advancement of computer technology. The prediction that Gordon Moore made in 1965 has held fairly true as of 2016. The rapid rate that computers are evolving at has allowed technology to advance as far as it has. It is very likely that Moore's law will continue for many years, allowing the technology to continue growing.

Quantum computers

At some point in time Moore's law is destined to run its course and the improvements in transistor-based computers will no longer be able to advance further. Electrical signals can only travel as fast as the speed of light. This limits both the size of computer and the frequency that they can operate at. Modern processors are capable of operating at frequencies above 4 billion cycles per second. In the amount of time that a processor goes through one cycle, light will only travel 3 inches. This limits the maximum length any possible signal path in the processor. This has been a known limitation of transistor-based computers for a long time. The way that processor technology has gotten around this hurdle is by making the individual transistors very small in size, which in turn allows for larger transistor networks or faster processing rates to be achieved.

As of 2016, processor technology has been shrunk down to 10nm for production chips. For this scale of chips, the smallest wire traces through the silicon are less than a hundred atoms wide. On a scale this small the material properties begin to act much less predictably, with particle physics beginning to interfere with the signals. One issue that is observed is quantum tunneling, which causes electrons to jump from one location to another and sometimes act as if they are in two locations at once, leading to false signals being recorded in calculations.

Quantum computers hold a unique ability to solve optimization problems due to the ability of particles to seemingly be in two locations at once. These optimization problems are some of the main problems experienced for aircraft control. For a drone to fly 5 packages to different locations there are 720 possible routes. As you add in more stops the number of possible routes goes up exponentially. Traditionally, a computer will have to calculate many possible solutions, compare their final states, and decide which is the best. For many problems not all possible solutions can be calculated in any reasonable amount of time, and large assumptions have to be made to narrow the range of results to be tested, which reduces the accuracy of the final result.

Quantum computers allow for problems to be evaluated in more efficient ways based on how the memory is being stored. Because a quantum bit can exist in two states at once the amount of data that an array of bits can store is 2^n, where n is the number of bits. For example, 40 quantum bits can store as much information at 1 trillion traditional bits. Processing is handled in a similar way as well, where vastly more information is processed in a single cycle. Google has tested quantum computers and these claims in their labs and have measured performance increases of 100 million times compared to a tradition computer[v]. Once this technology becomes better understood it will allow for much better control of drones, allowing for far better path planning, course guidance and landing selection. Just as transistor technology obsoleted vacuum tube computing quantum computers will provide the next biggest improvement.

Advancements in sensors

Advanced computers and programming are not of much use unless they are paired with accurate sensors to gather data. The computer guidance of the Saturn 5 tracked a preplanned line based off of accelerometers and gyroscopes, cutting edge technology at the time. Drones for commercial use will need to include many more sensors to allow them to navigate and land. Some of the new sensors consist of stereovision and LIDAR that give drones the sense of sight.

Stereovision is a type of sensor that uses two cameras in a manner similar to the human eyes. By comparing two images that are taken a certain distance apart the computer can process how far away objects are. Stereovision sensors are best suited for close range distances, less than 10 meters. Because they compare many points on an image at once they can achieve a high rate of point location. Industry leading sensors from Carnegie Robotics can define 11 million new points every second. These current sensors are large in size, and mainly developed for use in self driving vehicles[vi]. For these sensors to become widely used in drones the individual image sensors will need to be shrunk down to a smaller size to allow better integration with the airframe of the drone.

LIDAR is a laser based distance measurement device that pulses a laser beam in a direction, and measures the time that it takes for the beam to bounce back. In comparison to stereovision LIDAR offers a much larger range, at the expense of finding fewer points per second. Industry leading LIDAR offers a range of 100m and can define 25,000 points per second[vii].

LIDAR scan of a house on a street

A combination of many different types of sensors is necessary to control the drones. GPS will be relied upon for long distance navigation due to its absolute accuracy. When drones are flying close to terrain the LIDAR will generate a map of the drone's surroundings. And, for maneuvers requiring precise control such as landing, stereovision will provide a much greater volume of data to work with. As drones integrate with society they will operate in increasing close proximity to humans which will necessitate precision flying and awareness. Accurate and fast responding sensors such as LIDAR and stereovision provide improvements in sensor technology needed to accomplish these goals.

Humanitarian uses for drones

There are many humanitarian uses for drones. Their ability to access remote areas, carry payloads, and do so without human interaction will allow them to perform roles from wild fire spotting to emergency medical services.

Wildfire discovery and suppression

Wildfire observation and response is a field that will see vast improvements in effectiveness and safety from the use of drones. Wildfires are hard to observe due to the remoteness of many forests. In the 1900's the U.S. forest service built numerous fire lookouts on top of ridges and mountains. These were–staffed by forest service personnel. When a fire was detected they would relay the information to the main offices. The main offices would then coordinate an effort to put out the wildfire.

The amount of effort that went into preventing wildfires was justified due to the damage that they cause. From the year 2,000 to 2,015 over 250 lives have been lost to wildfires[viii]. In addition to the loss of life, wildfires destroy large amount of houses and property every year. The 2003 San Diego wildfires cost the county 2.45 billion dollars[ix]. With a large economic incentive to suppress wildfires before they grow too large there will certainly be funding to develop and maintain automated suppression systems.

For personal on the ground there is great danger involved in stopping the fire. Many of the techniques used to stop fires include cutting down trees and removing vegetation to create a fire break, a strip of land with all of the combustible material removed. Pilots will fly aircraft and helicopters over the fire to dump water and fire retardants over the area, skimming the surface of lakes to gather more water.

The main issues associated with the current standards for firefighting revolve around the safety of the operations as well as their effectiveness at stopping the fires. The system of forests in the U.S. is too large to be monitored by a few people in lookout towers. Once a fire is detected it can take many days for a response to be coordinated. This time allows the fire to grow larger, which increases the difficulty of extinguishing it.

Drones will be used to monitor and extinguish wildfires for many reasons, some of which being their ability to form large networks, work in close formations, find optimal solutions, and quick response times. The network of drones would function in a way similar to that of a swarm of insects. This style of having the drones communicate with each other and formulate their actions on their own allows for large tasks to be conducted without relying on constant human input or monitoring.

In a future where wildfires are fought with drones many different variants will be built to accomplish different tasks. The first variant will be scouting drones. These will be small in size, and built in large quantities. The role of these drones will be to keep eyes on the large areas covered in forests. These drones will utilize solar panels to be self-sufficient. When their batteries run low they will find a suitable landing space, land, and allow their internal batteries to recharge. These drones will be equipped with infrared cameras and sensors, and be able to detect fires as they are just starting.

When the drones are launched they will form packs that are assigned a certain area of forest. Sharing a common landing zone and task they will fly in rotations as close to nonstop as possible. The nonstop flights are key as they allow for early detection. The early detection drones will take on a VTOL design allowing them to take off from small clearings and transition to efficient forward flight to cover vast distances.

The second key type of drone will be the heavy lifter of the system, the fire extinguishing drones. These will be on standby the majority of the time, waiting for a call to action. These drones will be much larger VTOL aircraft, comparable in size and configuration to a V-22 osprey (a twin rotor-propeller aircraft with a 46 foot wingspan); they will have large cargo reserves for carrying water. When these aircraft are called into action they will need to operate continuously until the fire is put out. Due to this limitation electrical power is not ideal. Drones powered off of gas turbine engine will have an increased range and will be able to refuel quickly.

These aircraft will require much more maintenance than the early alert drones. They will be stationed at major airfields close to large forests. When they are called into action the drones will fly to a staging area close to the fire. This will consist of a large field that will become useful for refueling. As drones fly to the scene they will carry external fuel tanks to be left at the base. After the fuel is dropped off the aircraft will plot routes to the nearest lake and fill up with water. From there they will fly cycles to drop water on the fire. Once they are low on fuel they will refill from the tank they set down earlier. This close refueling station could triple the amount of flights the drones are capable of before they need to return to their home base.

Search and Rescue

Once a wildfire observation network is in place it will serve another important role for society, search and rescue. The high precision thermal sensors that will allow for drones to seek out wildfires will allow for these drones to very quickly locate people in a forest.

When a hiker goes missing, the drones will begin to keep a record of people in its location. From there search and rescuers will know which trails to check for the missing person or group. If the stranded people are in a remote location that rescue personnel can't reach soon enough a viable option exists to use another drone to fly the lost people supplies to help them survive, and instructions on how to use them.

Farming information systems

Farmers in the modern era are looking for ways to increase the quality of their crops, and to be more efficient with resources. Drones will help revolutionize the way that farming is conducted. Drones will fly many flights each day above the farm. Thermal imaging can be used to determine the moisture content of the soil. The more advanced levels of sensors will be able to use infrared imaging to make assumptions about crop quality.

This information will be sent to a computer that decides which areas of plants need water, fertilizers and other actions in order to get the best crops. From here the data will be sent to automated systems that will perform the desired function to the plants.

Civil Engineering Surveying

Drones will initiate big changes to how construction projects are planned and carried out. Civil engineering decisions often strive to be efficient with time, money and resources. A planned bridge should be placed in the ideal location to minimize the length of the span. Dams are built to maximize the water height for a given volume of the dam structure. Power transmission lines are constructed with the least effort to create a reliable system.

Drones offer surveyors a much greater freedom of where the sensors can go. A power transmission line that crosses a mountain range could be optimized to consider the large-scale geographic features, such as mountains and ridges, as well as the smaller scale geographic features, such as tree coverage and ground support. Drones will be able to be deployed to survey large amounts of land testing everything from soil stability to foliage coverage in remote areas that would be difficult to reach on foot. This increase in the amount of gathered information will be used to make better design decisions, which will result in cheaper projects that function better.

Power Line Inspection

The power line infrastructure in the U.S. is vast and complicated. Containing more than 300,000 miles of lines monitoring the system is a great task[x]. System monitoring is necessary for several reasons.

Power lines and their towers are out in the elements without a break. Overtime the structures will weaken and need to be replaced. With most towers sitting closer than a mile apart the number of towers that need to be inspected over time is very large. Power companies will use drones to inspect these lines due to the drones near continuous operation, lower operating costs compared to people, and reduced liability.

The drones will be built with power converters to allow them to recharge off of the lines as they travel. The ability to recharge from the lines will allow them to potentially cover thousands of miles of cable without straying from their tasks. In this situation the drones will be far more cost effective to a company compared to using people to do the inspections. Inspectors would have to drive from their home offices out to the power lines and back every day, or live on the road. Either of these options leads to a high cost for the company compared to the work being done.

Another benefit to the companies using drones is a reduction in liability. Tower climbers are among the riskiest jobs in America. With wrongful death settlements being very expensive for the company it is financially beneficial to remove workers from risky situations, aside from the ethical reasons to do so.

There are several limitations at the current time for this technology to be fully viable. After the drone gets to its tower to service, or line to inspect it needs to be capable of determining the structural soundness of the tower or cable. The majority of cross-country towers are made out of steel, which has a tendency to rust. One option for inspecting the metal would be to measure the reflectivity of the structure at different points. Areas that are rusted will show lower reflectivity values, and would trigger an alarm. The information of rust, along with laser scans of the tower can then be relayed to an operations center where employees will determine if a fix is necessary or not.

Medical response

In 2014 engineering students at the Technical University of Delft designed a drone to deliver defibrillators to reduce response time. The drone weighs 8 pounds, navigates off of GPS and can find the patient from their cell signal[xi]. Chief engineer Alex Monmont explains that the drone can deliver a defibrillator in less than a minute to any location in a 12 square kilometer area. Currently the survival rates for cardiac arrest are around 8%, and brain death can occur within 4-6 minutes[xii]. The TU Delft's drone is a great pioneer in the medical industry. In the following years these drones will be more common and take on more roles, providing emergency medication.

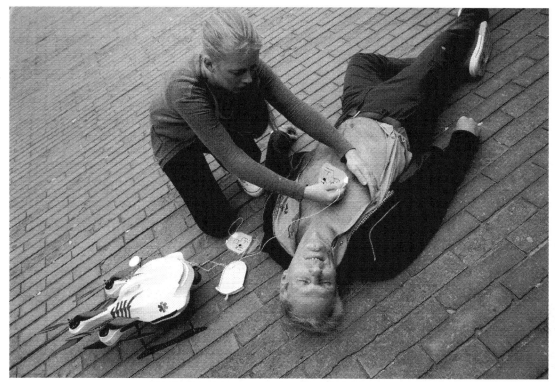
TU Delft's drone responds with a defibrillator

Future drones will need to be widespread and dependable so that one can be quickly dispatched to nearly any location at a moment's notice. The Portland metropolitan area covers an area of over 17,000 square kilometers. With TU Delft's drone technology over 1,300 drones will be needed to cover the Portland area. These drones will need to be spaced evenly to be efficient with coverage. Getting the drones to their optimal arrangement will most likely rely on the cooperation of residents and building owners to allow some of their land or roof space to house a drone.

There is room for improvement on the medical features that TU Delft's drone delivers. Right now the drone mainly focuses on treating cardiac arrest. A major source of accidents in the U.S. is the roadways and highway systems. Medical response will often take a long time on a highway because an ambulance will have to drive out to the location. Adding a trauma kit to the drones would allow them to take on roles of highway response as well. Liquid bandage and gauze will provide a quick means of stopping blood loss. The drones will also include personal protective equipment for the bystanders to use while treating the victim.

Due to the reliance on bystanders it will be highly beneficial to the program to incorporate medical training into the driver's license program or school system. An emergency response course would teach participants emergency means of stopping blood loss and treating shock. This preexisting knowledge, along with having a dispatch officer on speaker will help to guide the bystanders through any emergency procedures.

Because the medical use of drones relies heavily on bystanders taking a role in helping the victim better clarification of the Good Samaritan laws will encourage more people to take action. Good Samaritan laws exist in all 50 states to some extent. They serve to protect people who help in good faith and without gross negligence from liability lawsuits pertaining to their actions. In a society increasingly fearful of liability clarifying that accident responders are immune to lawsuits will increase the likelihood that bystanders step in to treat the victim.

Zipline's drone parachutes medicine into remote regions in Africa

Along with being first responders to an accident drones will also be used to quickly transfer medical equipment from one location to another. California startup company Zipline has been testing drones in remote areas of Rwanda as of 2015[xiii]. The drones are a 22lb airplane configuration and can fly supplies from larger medical facilities to much smaller rural centers. This is helping to increase the quality of care that the average citizen is able to attain. When a person becomes injured they will go to their local doctor. These local doctors do not have the resources to keep different types of blood on hand or to stock medicines. The doctor will use an app that contacts a Zipline station and a drone flies over and parachutes a package down to the ground. The Zipline drones are currently limited to a 35 mile operating radius, mainly due to the current drone design. As the range improves in the future this service will allow many more doctors to receive the supplies that they need to do their job.

Package delivery drones

Amazon was one of the first companies to sell products online, starting out with books in 1994. One of the ways that Amazon has stayed competitive in their market is that they continue to work with the cutting edge of technology to improve and streamline their process, making it easier for customers to purchase products online. As of 2016 Amazon's warehouses use complex computer algorithms to maximize packing efficiency of shelves, allowing them greater storage efficiency. This technical outlook by the company has lead them to create their own package delivery system for the 21st century.

Due to Amazon's heavy reliance on the shipping industry automated package delivery systems are a prime goal for the company. If Amazon can come up with a revolutionary package delivery system that is cost efficient and hassle free for consumers it will boost their sales, drive more people to their website, and reduce their dependence on other companies.

In 2013 Amazon CEO Jeff Bezos announced a plan that involved focusing on drone delivery for the US market. Testing under very controlled conditions has begun in 2015[xiv]. Amazon is not the only company that is pursuing the use of drones for delivery; DHL has worked on projects in Germany for general package delivery in the Bavarian mountains. This section will mainly focus on package delivery in the U.S. with its laws, and Amazon as a company, due to their very public presence.

Initial Amazon drone design, a multirotor system

The current system for receiving packages in the US involves a package delivery company bringing the package all the way to your doorstep. By the year 2025 self driving vehicles will be commonplace in society; however they will not be the best option for package delivery, due to one key challenge, getting the package from the truck to the doorstep. There are many different ways houses are designed. Some houses have doors at curb height, others have a step or two, and some have flights of steps. If self driving trucks are used the most viable method to get the package to the door is a bipedal robot that can access these areas as humans do. Simply leaving the package at the curb will not suffice for many people, as package theft is a large problem in certain neighborhoods.

Aerial vehicles can precisely time their delivery. With Amazon air you can select a product to be delivered in 30 minutes or less. This control over the time lets you be at home to receive the package yourself, a luxury that traditional package delivery does not offer.

Aerial vehicles can fly to the target location based off of GPS guidance and sense and avoid flight controllers. Once a drone gets to a house it will use machine-learned algorithms to decide the best spot for the package. LIDAR scanners will recognize large level fields and patios, while vision recognition can watch for people who may get too close to the drone for their safety.

Ideal configurations for package delivery drones are VTOL aircraft. Taking off and landing vertically will allow them to descend between a clearing of trees to reach a person's back yard and to land in the distribution center. VTOL aircraft are also able to make emergency landings in just about any space. In the event that a technical failure occurs and the aircraft is no longer airworthy it can set itself down in a small area free of people. An airplane would need to search for a much larger area to land at.

Rendering of the second generations of Amazon drones, a VTOL aircraft.

Once the aircraft has taken off it needs to fly to its destination. Helicopters and quadcopters generally have very low flight times compared to an airplane of similar weight. Having a VTOL aircraft allows for it to fly like a plane for a large distance in a very efficient manner.

Limiting Regulations
The U.S. has a very dense set of regulations on aircraft that have been put together by the FAA. These regulations take a long time to change and are one of the biggest limiting factors keeping the drone delivery industry from taking off. As of 2015 the FAA would not allow any UAS to be flown beyond the line of sight of its pilot, a very limiting rule that still stands to this day. One of the more restrictive limitations enforces a max vehicle weight limit of 55 pounds[xv]. This greatly limits the functionality of the package delivery drones, as tradeoffs have to be made that reduce either the package weight or flight distance.

Amazon has decided that the best combination of package and drone weight is a 50 pound drone carrying a 5 pound package. Packages under 5 pounds are the majority of the packages Amazon sells, and the drones are able to deliver the packages to anywhere within 15 miles of a fulfillment center with the package[xvi].

In order for the drone package delivery model to become widespread Amazon will need to extend the range that its drones are capable of flying. To get a package delivered by drone the item needs to be at a local fulfillment center within the range of the drone. In order to increase coverage Amazon needs drones with greater range, or more package fulfillment centers. Simply adding package fulfillment centers is not a viable long-term solution because the center needs to stock the item to be delivered adding more fulfillment centers increases the stock that Amazon needs for each item.

There are many measures that can be used to improve the functionality of the drone package delivery system. One of these factors is the payload capacity that the drones are capable of lifting. Currently drones are lifting 5 pound packages in the U.S. as regulations allow for larger drones the max package weight will increase. The key specification for package delivery is the drones range. Drones will need to advance from their 15 mile effective range to close to 50 miles. A 50 mile range will allow one major fulfillment center to deliver packages to the metropolitan area of any large city and its suburbs. If drones can achieve this range the package delivery idea can become reality.

In order to increase the range of the drones they will need to grow bigger. Larger drones allow for more batteries, packages, or fuel to be carried. This will allow the drones to deliver heavier packages a further distance. The first step in order to increase the size of the drones requires the FAA rewriting the rules of the air. The FAA's regulations were created for manned aircraft, and would require significant rework, if not starting over, to accommodate drones into the U.S. airspace. At first regulations will be made to allow unmanned aircraft to fly with close proximity to the ground, and out of the way of manned aircraft. Overtime these regulations will grow to allow larger flying aircraft to fly freight between cities, using the same airspace as manned aircraft.

Privacy Concerns

Concerns exist over the collection and use of data that the drones are gathering. Drones will have GPS sensors and cameras to guide themselves to a home[xvii]. It would be beneficial for package delivery companies to retain as much information as possible to improve their maps and aid in future deliveries. Tech companies have gotten criticized in the past for data retention policies. Google street view, a service that allows people to view a series of photos taken down most streets has faced criticism for the information that it has gathered. Despite all the photos being gathered legally from public roads there has been a backlash that the information gathering is intruding too far[xviii]. Once drones begin to fly over people's back yards to deliver packages this data collection will become a bigger issue.

In order for the public to trust the package delivery drones there will need to be oversight into how this information is used. It may be decided that the information should only be used temporarily, and removed from the drone after each flight. A much more intrusive decision would be that the data can be used for any company and any use. A lot will be at stake for deciding these boundaries. According to the wall street journal online advertising brought in revenue of over 50 billion dollars in 2015[xix]. The online add market is driven by targeted ads. These ads have generated controversy around their use. Targeted ads work by gathering information about a person and putting together a profile of their interests. A person who has a history of purchasing knitting supplies will be more likely to be influenced on an ad for yarn, than someone who is interested in cars. Websites use information about your searches and shopping habits to show you ads that you are likely to respond favorably to. As drones take on more roles for society and provide more services. It is important that a close eye is kept on the use of personal data.

Package delivery drones will become more popular in the next decade. They offer a quick way for packages to be delivered and there will always be people willing to pay a premium to get something quick. Valid concerns do exist over privacy and how this technology may intrude into people's lives. With future testing and a resolution to the concerns that are raised drone package delivery will eventually become a staple of the online shopping system.

Looking to the future

Fully automated flight controls are still in the developmental phase. Each year computers, sensors, and algorithms improve to allow drones to be more stable in flight, avoid obstacles, and carry out their assigned task. As these technologies keep advancing into the future drones will become ubiquitous with society, and take on more tasks. The majority of these tasks will increase the quality of life of those who they affect; however, some uses for drones are not without their concerns. Privacy has been a great concern with the advancements and popularity of computers. Having computers flying over your house with cameras on should be a concern to many. Inevitably, as people push back against the idea of drones, companies will be forced to take a stance on privacy and inform the public on their actions.

Along with improvements in technology, improvements will have to be made to the laws and regulations that govern the industry. Much of the laws that exist as of 2016 have been designed with the sole consideration of human piloted aircraft. These laws often follow the direction of industry, and as more companies produce and operate drones the FAA will have to reconsider their stance, as it would take close to a complete refresh of laws to incorporate manned and unmanned aircraft in a way to allow both to perform optimally.

Our grandchildren will experience a different life than we will. My grandparents experienced the invention and rise of the television, computers, the space race, refrigerators and more. For many of us, our whole lives we have looked up at the sky and seen contrails from jets shuttling people around the world. Our grandchildren will live in a world where drones are used for package delivery, for emergency medical response, for crop monitoring, and many more uses. Most of the uses will bring about positive changes in their lives; improving survival for many medical conditions, increased crop health and food supply, and mitigating the consequences of environmental disaster. For them, looking up and seeing drones will be a part of their lives, something that they have never lived without. Drones will be an accepted tool of their society that increases their quality of life.

[i] 11/12/2016, drone, Dictionary.com, http://www.dictionary.com/browse/drone.

ii X-47B UCAS, NorthropGrumman.com,
http://www.northropgrumman.com/capabilities/x47bucas/documents/ucas-d_data_sheet.pdf.

iii 11/12/2016, Saturn Launch Vehicle Digital Computer, Wikipedia.com,
https://en.wikipedia.org/wiki/Saturn_Launch_Vehicle_Digital_Computer.

iv 11/12/2016, Moore"s Law, Wikipedia.com, https://en.wikipedia.org/wiki/Moore%27s_law.

v Aron, J.,11/14/2016, Quantum computer firm D-Wave claims massive performance boost,
NewScientist.com, https://www.newscientist.com/article/dn28078-quantum-computer-firm-d-wave-claims-massive-performance-boost/.

vi 11/12/2016, Products, CarnegieRobotics.com, http://carnegierobotics.com/products/.

vii 11/13/2016, World"s Smartest Long-Range 3D LIDAR is Released: RobotEye RE08,
OcularRobotics.com, http://www.ocularrobotics.com/re08-3d-laser-scanner/.11/13/2016,

viii 11/12/2016, Wildland Fire Fatalities by Year, NIFC.gov,
https://www.nifc.gov/safety/safety_documents/Fatalities-by-Year.pdf.

ix Diaz, J.,11/12/2016, Economic Impacts of Wildfire, FireAdaptedNetwork.com,
https://fireadaptednetwork.org/wp-content/uploads/2014/03/economic_costs_of_wildfires.pdf.

x 11/14/2016, What is the electric power grid and what are some challenges it faces, EIA.gov,
http://www.eia.gov/energy_in_brief/article/power_grid.cfm.

xi 11/12/2016, Ambulance Drone" Could Drastically Increase Heart Attack Survival, IFLScience.com,
http://www.iflscience.com/health-and-medicine/ambulance-drone-could-drastically-increase-heart-attack-survival/.

xii 11/12/2016, Ambulance Drone with Integrated Defibrilator, UASVision.com,
http://www.uasvision.com/2014/10/29/ambulance-drone-with-integrated-defibrillator/.

xiii Toor, A.,11/12/2016, Drones will begin delivering blood and medicine in the US, TheVerge.com,
http://www.theverge.com/2016/8/2/12350274/zipline-drone-delivery-us-launch-blood-medicine.

xiv 11/12/2016, Amazon Unveils Futuristic Plan: Delivery by Drone, CBSNews.com,
http://www.cbsnews.com/news/amazon-unveils-futuristic-plan-delivery-by-drone/.

xv 11/12/2016, Summary of Small Unmanned Aircraft Rule, FAA.gov,
https://www.faa.gov/uas/media/Part_107_Summary.pdf.

xvi Soper, T.,11/12/2016, Amazon reveals new delivery drone design with range of 15 miles,
GeekWire.com, http://www.geekwire.com/2015/amazon-releases-updated-delivery-drone-photos-video-showing-new-prototype/.

xvii 11/14/2016, Amazon Prime Air, Wikipedia.com,
https://en.wikipedia.org/wiki/Amazon_Prime_Air#cite_note-Schlag.2C_Chris_2013-10.

xviii Helft, M.,11/12/2016, Google Zooms In Too Close for Some, NYTimes.com,
http://www.nytimes.com/2007/06/01/technology/01private.html.

xix Marshall, J.,11/14/2016, U.S. Internet Ad Revenues Grew 19% During First Half of 2015, WSJ.com,
http://www.wsj.com/articles/u-s-internet-ad-revenues-grew-19-during-first-half-of-2015-1445439603.

CHAPTER 7:

WILL WE EVER BE ABLE TO FLY EVERYWHERE?

THE FUTURE OF PERSONAL AIR VEHICLES

Justin Inman, Senior

Mechanical, Industrial and Manufacturing Engineering

What is a Personal Air Vehicle (PAV)?

More than one hundred years have passed since humans figured out how to get a heavier than air, powered, and controllable flying machine into the air. More than one hundred years of research, engineering, analysis, testing, and design evolution, have all contributed to the maturity of vehicles that fly through the air. The magic of flight has moved us as a species to reach higher and farther faster and safer than we ever have been able to do in history both in wartime and in peacetime. However, throughout the century, there has been a segment of the aviation industry that has captured the heart of designers and the general public alike, but that has not come to be mainstream or even past proving stages. Many have tried, yet none have really succeeded although this idea has existed since the earliest aviation pioneers. That idea is the Personal Air Vehicle (PAV).

The definition of a PAV has constantly evolved over the years, following new discoveries in aircraft design, power, and materials. As the aviation industry has advanced technologically, new doors have opened for the PAV, each one looking more promising than the last, but all invariably falling short. Of the many modern definitions of the PAV, the highly respected definition created by the Comparative Aircraft Flight Efficiency (CAFÉ) Foundation is the most holistic definition for what a PAV will look like in the future.

The CAFÉ Foundation definition for a PAV outlines eight points that define PAV regarding performance, autonomy, safety, and mainstream public integration. The points are: [1]

1. 150-200 mph "car" that flies above gridlock traffic without delays
2. Quiet, safe, comfortable and reliable
3. Simplified operation akin to driving a car
4. As affordable as travel by car or airliner
5. Near all-weather, on demand travel enabled by synthetic vision
6. Highly energy-efficient and non-polluting
7. Up to 800 mile range
8. Short runway use – (Walk to Grandma's from small residential airfields)

This list, although seemingly simple at first glance, defines an engineering and social puzzle that has been historically impossible to solve.

Why does the general public need or want PAVs, and why have aircraft designers dreamed of creating PAVs for so many years? Besides the fact that there is something magical about flight, the idea of eliminating traffic congestion on roads has long been an appealing aspect of the PAV. Instead of traveling in an automobile on the two-dimensional surface of the earth while constrained by barriers, lane markings, and other automobiles trying to hit you, the PAV would travel in three dimensions (think stacking traffic directions at different altitudes) and could travel point to point instead of being constrained to roads. Without analyzing too much the mess that this system of mass PAV use would make of the world's airspace systems, it's great to think that road traffic congestion (and associated waste and pollution) could be eliminated or very much reduced with common PAV travel.

The CAFE foundation cites traffic congestion and the promise that PAVs can bring to reducing traffic congestion as one of the main motivators for development of the PAV. [2]

> *Gridlocked highways increasingly burden our society. Currently, the doorstep-to-doorstep average speed for cars is 35 mph. In the greater Los Angeles area, this speed is predicted to degrade to just 22 mph by year 2020. Even today in peak traffic periods a trip through the Los Angeles or San Francisco freeway system to any destination within 100 miles typically involves these low average speeds. Statistics show that, on average, cars carry only 1.3 people, even with High Occupancy Vehicle (HOV) lanes in place.*
>
> *The U.S. Department of Transportation (DOT) states that 6.7 billion gallons of gasoline are wasted in traffic jams each year. This is over 20 times more gasoline than is consumed by today's entire general aviation fleet. Also, the future system of travel by PAVs expressly avoids air traffic jams and can substantially help to relieve those on our highways. Michigan's DOT program manager states that moving just " 2 to 5 percent of the vehicles to underutilized routes, . . can dramatically reduce congestion." Mass transit can help reduce congestion, but it is typically underutilized because its convenience is inherently limited in both reach and scheduling.*

Not only does the PAV promise reduced traffic congestion, the PAV also offers the advantage of very fast trips. A PAV would travel in a straight line to a destination at 150-200 mph compared to an automobile traveling a non-straight line at 25-70 mph. The increased time savings of travel would be very attractive. However, this is 2016 and the PAV has not even hatched yet. So, while it is enjoyable to fantasize about the possibilities the PAV could afford to society, there is a long way to go.

So, when will we get the PAV? The answer is "It depends." The development of the PAV to fit the CAFÉ definition is dependent on many technologies, the largest of which is a suitable power plant. Will the PAV be mainstream by 2050? Based on the current level of maturity of the PAV and to what level of social and engineering/technical maturity the PAV will need to mature to in order to become mainstream, it is doubtful that the PAV will be mainstream by 2050. However, depending on the rate of maturation of technologies required for the PAV to fulfill its definition, the timeline for maturity of the PAV may be shorter or longer.

The CAFÉ Foundation weighs in on the timeline of the PAV with a perspective from NASA.[2]

> *NASA seems hopeful that the maturity of the PAV will happen within the next fifty years; even the next few years!*
>
> *NASA predicts that by 2020, up to 45% of all miles traveled may be in PAVs and that they will be the preferred way to travel for distances of 75 to 800 miles. [NASA PAV study] For Personal Air Vehicles to fulfill such a role , they must become attractive to consumers by demonstrating their safety, environmental-friendliness and cost-effective advantages over cars and airliners.*
>
> *The FAA's Joint Planning Development Office (JPDO) is already planning for PAVs to have a role in our future air transportation system. There is wide agreement at NASA, the National Research Council, and the American Institute of Aeronautics and Astronautics (AIAA) that industry and private innovators need a stimulus for the appropriate technologies to be converged into marketable PAVs. Fortunately, Congress has recognized that need and has authorized NASA to fund a cash technology prize to provide that stimulus. [NASA announcement] It is called the PAV Challenge and this essay explains why it is being called "NASA's Moonshot for Aeronautics."*

This excerpt was written circa 2005, which gave NASA and industry fifteen years to meet their 2020 projection. Seeing as how 2016 is almost over (meaning 2020 is only three years away) and there has been very little progress on the maturity of the PAV since 2005, it is extremely unlikely that NASA's claim that "45% of all miles traveled will be done in PAVs by 2020" will come to fruition.

There is no doubt however, that there will continue to be an interest in PAVs by designers, manufacturers, and the public as supporting technologies develop. The hope is that eventually the PAV will exist, and eventually the PAV will be mainstream. So, what needs to happen to get there? And what current foundation does the PAV have to build off of?

Offspring of General Aviation

The PAV is the ultimate evolution of, and solidly rooted in, general aviation. What is general aviation? At the end of WWII, thousands of pilots across the country (and around the world) found themselves without a way to fly. Many of these pilots had fallen in love with flying and wanted a personal flying vehicle they could use for pleasure flying. At the same time, aircraft manufacturers across the country (and around the world) found themselves without their largest customer: the military. These companies realized there were many surplus military pilots who wanted something to fly, so these companies developed small, one and two seat aircraft that were mass produced and affordable by a working-class man. That was what really kickstarted general aviation. General aviation aircraft followed the design and engineering progression of the commercial and military industry. These small aircraft steadily increased in power and performance over the decades and the materials used in construction of general aviation aircraft evolved from fabric-covered steel tube trusses, to aluminum airframes, to composite airframes.

General aviation is mostly comprised of hobbyists, people who own an aircraft for pleasure, because they can and want to. (A large segment of general aviation also includes flight training towards a career in airline flying. General aviation is where all pilots, excluding military pilots, learn to fly. However as this segment of general aviation is not directly related to personal flying and thus not directly related to the PAV, we will ignore it.) General Aviation aircraft are slightly practical for travel and can be used to privately fly long distances (think across countries) but doing so is normally more expensive than traveling by car or airline. New general aviation aircraft are also very expensive ($125,000 to $800,000).

No longer is a new airplane within the economic reach of the average working man. The high cost of acquisition and ownership for general aviation aircraft is partially driven by very stringent, time-intensive, and costly government certification regulations for an aircraft design. These certification requirements have stifled innovation in general aviation over the past thirty years and have resulted in high costs to manufacturers, which in turn result in high costs to consumers. The cost of general aviation has helped drive out the common man from privately owning an aircraft and created a public perception that aircraft = wealth = not attainable for me.

Enter the PAV. This world of stringent government regulations for general aviation private aircraft, high development costs, and low public interest is what the PAV will have to start with. The first PAVs will also have to operate in the modern national airspace system and abide by all the regulations relating to that airspace. Over time, as the PAV gains popularity, the regulations will slowly change to better apply to PAVs and uses of PAVs. Ultimately the groundwork for the PAV has been laid by general aviation. This groundwork will just need to change.

Flying Cars: A Historical Failure

A discussion of the PAV would not be complete without a brief aside about a type of PAV that has often been considered as the ultimate evolution of the PAV: the flying car. For many years designers and the general public thought that the future of personal air travel would be a one-stop-shop for all your driving and flying needs: a car that could fly or an airplane that could drive on the roads. The idea of flying cars has fascinated people since the beginnings of aviation when even the automobile was yet in its infancy. In fact, until recently, the definition of a PAV effectively was a flying car. The challenges of designing a practical flying car have proved to be almost insurmountable. Very few people have designed a flying car that can actually both fly and drive well, and no one has created a flying car reliable enough, practical enough, or affordable enough to become mainstream.

The most successful flying car ever made was created by Moulton Taylor. Named the *Aerocar*, this flying car (or roadable aircraft) flew for the first time in 1949. The *Aerocar* featured a small car-like body with wings and a tail boom where the propeller was mounted. In flying configuration, the wings and tail would fold into position and in driving configuration, the wings and tail could be manually disconnected and pulled behind the car as a trailer. Only six were ever made. Fast forward to the 21st century. There are only two well known companies with flying car prototypes that actually fly. One is the United States based Terrifuiga, and the other a Dutch company, PAL-V. As mentioned earlier, the certification requirements for general aviation aircraft are very onerous. The highway safety certification required for mass produced roadable vehicles is also onerous. Combine those two stringent certification requirements with the complexities of a vehicle that can transform between a roadable vehicle and an aircraft, and you get an engineering puzzle that hasn't been well-solved.

Looking at the definition of the PAV, a flying car does not really meet the requirements. Considering the historic failure of the flying car, it seems that the PAV is better off being strictly an air vehicle anyway, at least in its early stages. In fact, this is all that NASA and the CAFE Foundation have proposed. The flying car is an issue of trying to do too much at once. Combining the roadable aspect into a new aircraft technology is an extra step that does not need to exist to meet the definition of a PAV, and in the long run, the PAV industry will be better off without trying to start with flying cars.

If the PAV is not to be a flying car, what will it be like? Referring back to the CAFE foundation's definition of a PAV, we can figure out the categories in which the PAV will need to mature, technologically and socially.

Speed and Endurance

The CAFE definition of the PAV places rather strict and high reaching performance requirements on the PAV. The PAV must be "150-200mph 'car' that flies above gridlock without traffic delays" and must be able to have an "up to 800 mile range".

There are four main forces that act on an aircraft: Lift, weight, thrust, and drag. Lift makes an aircraft move upwards, while weight tries to pull it back to earth. Thrust pulls (or pushes) the aircraft through the air but drag resists that forward movement. In fact, as the speed of an aircraft increases, the drag of an aircraft increases with the square of the speed. In other words, every time the speed of an aircraft doubles, the drag pulling back on the aircraft quadruples.

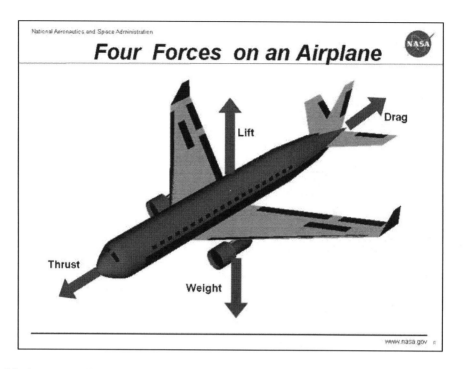

Four Forces on an Airplane

Lift

Drag

Thrust

Weight

Putting this in perspective of the PAV, the requirement that the PAV must be able to fly at speeds between 150-200 mph means that the PAV must be very streamlined and aerodynamic (meaning the air will flow over the aircraft without creating as much drag). Not only does the PAV have to travel at 150-200 mph, but it also needs to be able to sustain those speeds for 800 miles. At 200 mph, that means the PAV will need to be able to stay in the air for four hours, and at 150mph, the PAV will need to stay in the air for over five hours. These performance requirements require that the PAV have a very energy-efficient shape.

In addition to the aerodynamic efficiency that the PAV must have in order to help reduce aerodynamic drag, the PAV must also be as light as possible. If an aircraft is too heavy, it cannot fly well, and it will not be efficient. For the PAV to maintain 150-200 mph for over four hours, its weight must be kept to an absolute minimum. However, the PAV definition references the PAV to be a "car", which means that it will have the creature comforts that the general public has come to expect from modern automobiles. Comforts such as legroom, elbowroom, and nice comfortable interiors are wonderful to operate in but also add weight!

The aerodynamic design to keep the drag to a minimum, and the structural design to keep the weight to a minimum, will be the easiest part of the PAV maturity. In fact, it is currently possible to create such a structure using modern composite materials.

Materials used in aircraft construction are ever changing and becoming stronger and lighter. The materials used to build aircraft in fifty years will be even better suited for the PAV than the materials used today. Based on current and forthcoming materials, the structural and aerodynamic design of the PAV will not be the limiting factor in the PAVs maturity and success.

Although modern materials and aerodynamics are capable of creating a PAV that structurally meets the efficiency definition for a PAV, the biggest issue is what will power that structure. Something will need to be used to move the PAV structure through the air at 150-200 mph for

800 miles, but what will that be? The last performance-based requirement from the CAFÉ PAV definition is that a PAV must be "Highly energy efficient and non-polluting". Aerodynamic efficiency is important for satisfying this requirement, but must be paired with a power plant that is also highly energy-efficient and non-polluting. This rules out the internal combustion engine as a power plant. Ultimately this requirement is the sticky wicket preventing the PAV from maturing. There is just no power plant currently available that satisfies this requirement and also powers an aircraft at 150-200 mph for 800 miles.

Propulsion (the Weakest Link)

Electric power is currently the most popular technology choice and is highly touted as the future of aircraft and vehicle power. The drawback to electric power, though, is the batteries. Remember what weight does to an aircraft? Currently batteries do not have the power to weight ratio to make them a viable option for use in PAVs. Battery technology is slowly developing, and the energy density of batteries is slowly increasing. Although currently fueled by the emerging electric automobile industry, will batteries in their current form ever become a viable, practical option for the PAV? Based on the investment and current research into battery technology, it seems likely that batteries could become viable for use in the PAV. But will they? And how long will it take?

Another less popular form of electric power for aircraft is using a fuel cell to generate electricity to power an electric motor. However, again, the weight of this technology added to the unfriendly design requirements related to fuel cells (such as very high pressure tanks) make it a system unable to deliver the power and efficiency required to propel a PAV at 150-200 mph for 800 miles.

One of the benefits of an electric power plant is the possibility of changing the way the motors are used on the aircraft. Instead of using one main, large, motor (or engine) to drive a single propeller, the power consumption and efficiency characteristics of electric motors allow many smaller electric motors to be used without losing efficiency. This means that instead of mounting the motor and propeller only on the nose or tail of the PAV, many motors could be mounted along the forward edge of the wings, increasing the lift of the wings and the overall efficiency of the aircraft.

Looking ahead fifty years, there is a chance that the future of PAV power may not be centered around an electric motor at all. Perhaps another technology will be discovered and developed that will be perfectly suited for the PAV and its mission requirements.

Either way, a power plant technology will need to be developed that is capable of powering the PAV to meet its performance requirements while also being highly energy efficient and non-polluting. Unfortunately this is what will prevent the PAV from maturing within the next fifty years. However, who knows how fast power plant technology that will be well suited and viable for use in PAVs may develop.

Autonomy

Another facet of the PAV needed to satisfy the CAFÉ foundation PAV definition is automated systems. Automated systems will be responsible for the control and stability of the PAV as well as its navigation and integration into the national airspace system. As stated in the PAV requirements, a PAV must have "simplified operation akin to driving a car" and "near all-weather, on-demand travel enabled by synthetic vision". Automated systems will allow the PAV to operate as a fully autonomous vehicle as well as an assisted autonomous vehicle. This will assure a high level of operational safety and will also make a license to fly a PAV as easy to get as a driving license.

Currently it is very challenging to get a pilot certificate. There are very specific requirements related to hours of flight instruction in an aircraft that must be met before a person can receive their license to fly. This is because operating a general aviation aircraft is very different from operating an automobile. An aircraft opens up another dimension to explore, but also opens up another dimension that requires instruction on how to use safely.

If the PAV is to become a mainstream vehicle available and popularly used by the general public, the PAV will need to use computer-controlled automated systems to assist the human operator who is operating the PAV (assisted autonomous), or simply just operate itself with human observance but not necessarily human input (fully autonomous). Technology already exists that would be capable of completely controlling a PAV autonomously or assisting a human operator in the control of the aircraft. For the past twenty years, airliners have used autopilot technology that is advanced enough to be trusted to land aircraft with hundreds of people on board without human input in weather conditions deemed too dangerous for a human to land the aircraft. These systems require human supervision in the case of a computer or input failure, but do not use human control input.

General aviation has experienced an increase in available automated systems in the last twenty years. General aviation aircraft cannot land themselves as airliners can, but general aviation aircraft can still be programmed to fly any flight path including climbs, descents, and speed changes with the correct inputs. On the automated automobile side of things, companies such as TESLA have made advances in automated systems in the last ten years to where the automobile can operate itself with only human supervision in case of a malfunction or loss of sensor input, etc. In many ways, autonomous automobiles are harder than autonomous aircraft because automobiles are restricted by roads. Aircraft do not have the issue of running into barricades, pedestrians, or other vehicles.

It is true that as the PAV becomes more and more popular, air traffic congestion will become increasingly denser. But modern air traffic collision avoidance technology working in conjunction with air traffic controlling agencies and other autonomous aircraft will make air congestion a non-issue. The technology exists now that would allow the PAV to be either completely autonomous or autonomous enough that a human operator could "direct" the PAV after being trained in a simple "pilot training program," a program which would be no more complicated than earning a driving license.

If the operation of the PAV is to be assisted by a human operator, there needs to be a system for synthetic vision so that the human operator can "see" obstacles in the flight path. Although obstacle avoidance could very easily be achieved while operating fully autonomously without displaying anything on a screen, having a system for synthetic vision to allow the human operator to have situational awareness even in weather conditions where seeing the ground from the PAV is not possible, is important.

Just as the technology for automated control of a PAV exists presently, so does technology for synthetic vision. In fact, new general aviation aircraft come equipped with synthetic vision that is displayed on the flight instrumentation screens. This synthetic vision is derived from topographical data and drawn as three dimensional objects on the screen. Present day synthetic vision can also display obstacles and other aircraft on the screen.

Another benefit of a synthetic vision system is increased ease of navigation. To navigate the PAV, all the human operator will need to do is fly the PAV through a series of boxes drawn on the flight instrument screen which mark out the route to be flown. This system is called Highway-In-The-Sky (HITS) and gives aerial navigation video-game-like simplicity.

Another technology that will augment topographically mapped synthetic vision is forward-looking infrared. Once the PAV flies below a certain altitude when approaching a landing strip to land, the synthetic vision system will switch over to a video feed from a forward looking infrared system, allowing the human operator to see the landing strip even in very low visibility conditions (including the dark of night) and assist with the landing.

Although synthetic vision systems are common in new general aviation aircraft, the synthetic vision technology has not evolved to where synthetic vision can be used for primary aerial decision making. In fifty years, when used in PAVs, the synthetic vision will need to have evolved to where it can be used for primary flight navigation and aerial decision making. Synthetic vision and HITS will allow the PAV to seamlessly interface with the national airspace system and air traffic control system of the future. Flight routes will be sent to the PAV prior to departure and either the human operator or the PAV autonomously will fly the assigned routes.

Computer automation is presently capable of controlling a PAV and making a PAV easy for someone with minimal training to safely operate. Borrowing advances in technology from the autonomous automobile industry, the technology used to control and augment control of the first PAVs will be very capable. Since the autonomous technology is ready now, whenever PAV finally hatches, autonomous technology will be very well suited for use in PAVs.

Operational Infrastructure

One of the allures and defining traits of the PAV is "Short runway use – (Walk to Grandma's from small residential airfields)." This adds another nontechnical dimension to the maturity of the PAV and that is the implementation of infrastructure to support ownership and operation of a PAV. There are over 5000 paved airfields in the United States alone and over 9000 non-paved airfields. Most of the paved airfields are public use whereas many of the non-paved airfields are used for private operations.

When PAVs begin to mature to where they are attainable for some of the public, more airfields will need to be constructed to support the increased demand for landing places. Creating residential airfields and airfields close to malls and shopping centers will be costly in the beginning but will be necessary to increase the practicality of PAVs. There will need to be partnerships between cities and PAV manufacturers and government subsidies for cities to implement a few PAV specific airfields when the PAV is beginning to become common.

These airfields will consist of a few hundred feet of paved landing strip surrounded by garages to store the PAVs when not in use. Because it will not be possible to have small airfields everywhere initially, the airfields will need to be located near attractions such as restaurants, shopping centers, and hotels. Ride-share programs could also become popular at these airfields where an electric automobile is used to drive a couple miles from the airfield to someone's home or a certain store. Having a network of small airfields including residential airfields (where houses with garages for PAVs are connected by a series of taxiways to a common community airfield shared by the neighborhood) would allow the PAV to be integrated into day to day travel. Including trips across town (or even across state) to within walking distance Grandma's house.

Developing this infrastructure for use by PAVs cannot happen until early PAVs are already in production. Electric automobiles have followed this progression, where the early production electric automobiles did not have the infrastructure to support their operation over any large distances or even for long trips across town. It wasn't until the electric automobile began to get popular that the infrastructure for charging electric cars began to be implemented everywhere. This is a hard paradox. Implementation and popularity of a new technology such as the PAV will not increase unless there is infrastructure to support it and make it practical. In the same way, the infrastructure to support and make PAVs practical will not increase unless the PAV becomes a popular vehicle. Regardless of how the infrastructure to support PAV operations is implemented, as the PAV matures to where it can be mass produced, the infrastructure will follow.

Not Just Technological

The biggest technological hurdle keeping the PAV from maturing is the lack of a suitable power plant capable of delivering practical performance and efficiency. But the technological barriers keeping the PAV from maturing are not the only barriers that the PAV will need to overcome before it can become a household commodity. The PAV will need to overcome the general public's opinion of flying, especially flying in a "small plane."

Fear of flying has been a public issue since the beginning of the airplane. There is something about hurtling through thin air a few miles above the ground at speeds greater than anyone would drive a car that makes people uncomfortable and scared. Even with modern airliners in the United States, a passenger transportation system that has had zero fatal accidents directly related to flying since 2009, people are still afraid to fly.

On a slightly different level, the public sees general aviation airplanes as dangerous, foolhardy, and scary. Although the fatal accident record for general aviation is nowhere near as clean as the fatal accident record for airlines, the chances of dying in a general aviation airplane are significantly lower than the chances of dying in an automobile.

The public's psychological fear of flying will be something that PAV will need to break through if the PAV is ever to be successful. The requirement for PAVs to be "quiet, safe, comfortable, and reliable" speaks directly to those fears. While the PAV will be born into the world of general aviation, the PAV will also be its own new and novel technology. As such, it will be important for the PAV to make continuously good public impressions from its earliest stages.

Keeping the Neighbors Happy

It will be important for PAVs to be quiet. As the PAV starts to become mainstream and more and more PAVs are used in day-to-day travel, the sky will become very active very quickly. The noise generated by a vastly increased number of aircraft is a veritable concern for some people. General aviation airplanes in the United States are currently not required to meet any regulations regarding noise. A general aviation aircraft can be very loud, and many are very loud. However, in European countries, general aviation aircraft are required to meet stringent noise regulations designed to keep air traffic noise to a minimum. Many people in the United States do not like airplane noise and wish the United States government would enact rules to limit the amount of noise allowed for general aviation aircraft.

Because it will be important for the PAV to make a good public impression from its earliest stages, the PAV will need to be quiet. Making PAVs quiet will not be hard to do. If electric power is what ends up powering the PAV, a positive characteristic of electric power is low noise emission. Combining quiet electric power with aerodynamically engineered and optimized propellers will allow the PAV to be a friendly neighbor and will make it more attractive to people who would spurn noisy aircraft.

Proving Reliability and Building a Good Reputation

Safe, comfortable, and reliable, are qualities that work hand-in-hand. These three qualities are the most important aspects for the general public when buying any vehicle. In order for the general public to see the PAV as safe, it will need to be proven safe through testing and will need to "feel" safe psychologically.

Testing is the only way to prove a new technology. When a suitable power plant matures enough for practical use in PAVs, the companies that make the PAVs will need to perform countless hours of testing: testing to prove that the power plant is reliable, testing to prove that the aerodynamics and structure are safe, testing to prove that the computer flight automation can control the aircraft safely, testing to prove performance claims, and testing to prove crash safety. All this testing will need to be performed before the public accepts the PAV as safe and reliable. Once these few people accept the PAV as safe and reliable, and after these people purchase a PAV, and after these people operate their PAVs, proving them to be safe and reliable, only then will the general public accept the PAV as safe and reliable.

Comfort directly influences psychological safety. The seats and interior of PAVs will be designed to make the human occupants relaxed. People who are relaxed generally feel safer and more at ease. Restraint systems such as seat belts will give the human occupants an additional sense of safety.

Ultimately, the PAV will need to build its own reputation as a vehicle that is quiet, safe and reliable. It must build this reputation. Failure to build this reputation could easily result in PAV technology technically matured but not mainstream because of public perception. A touchy business indeed.

Affordable and Attainable

The last PAV requirement is that travel by PAV must be "as affordable as travel by car or airliner." Initially this requirement seems unattainable. However, based on the performance aspects of the PAV, achieving traveling costs equivalent to travel by car or airliner should not be difficult. Because of the highly energy efficient and non-polluting nature of the PAV power plant, the cost of operating a PAV should be very minimal.

Assuming electric power using highly efficient batteries as the storage for that power, the largest operating cost would be the price of the electricity used to charge the batteries. The large cost will be in initial acquisition. The early PAVs will be very expensive and not attainable by the general public.

However, this is expected of any new cutting edge technology. Flat screen televisions were only financially attainable by wealthy individuals for many years until the demand for the product and the technology and manufacturing processes and techniques evolved to the point where prices could come down. The present electric automobile industry is a good example of this initial high price. For many years, electric automobiles that are practical to operate in terms of range and comfort have been financially attainable only by relatively wealthy individuals. In the next two years, there will be electric automobiles that will incorporate practical range, comfort, and speed in a package financially attainable by the average working man. The PAV will undoubtedly follow a similar progression once mature enough for production. Ultimately though, the PAV will be as expensive to initially acquire as an automobile but will be less expensive to operate.

If the maturity of the PAV is being hindered by the lack of a suitable power plant, and if the public has a perception that small flying vehicles are dangerous, what else can happen to grow interest in the PAV, change the public opinion, and perhaps even accelerate the maturity of a suitable power plant so that the PAV may mature in the next half-century (or ever)?

Creating Enamorment

The general public and aircraft designing and manufacturing companies need to become more enamored with the PAV. One of the best catalysts for development and maturity of a new technology is competition. Private companies, industry associations, and governments will need to hold challenges and prizes as an incentive for designers and manufacturers to "prove themselves." These challenges also capture the eye of the public.

Positive media attention on these competitions and challenges would also help change the public's opinion about PAVs and increase their "cool factor". The idea of accelerating a new technology through competition is nothing new. In the 1930s Charles Lindbergh flew by himself nonstop, in a single engine airplane across the Atlantic Ocean from the United States to France. By doing so he set a record and also won a competition which made him some money and lots of fame.

His transatlantic flight was not just a spontaneous decision to fly by himself across the Atlantic Ocean. In the months prior to his flight, he had partnered with a United States based aircraft manufacturer to design and build a one-off purpose built aircraft specifically for that flight. By successfully completing that transatlantic flight, Charles Lindbergh helped advance and prove the technology of a single engine airplane and also impress and enamor the general public.

Similar records and competitions have been set throughout aviation history. Records such as supersonic flight, private space flight, and most recently electric flight are common. Each competition and each record helps prove a certain technology and positively influences the general public's opinion towards that technology.

Accelerating Maturity

Government incentives such as manufacturing subsidies could help speed up the maturity and development of the PAV as well as the public infrastructure to support frequent PAV operations. The military could also contract with private PAV companies or develop PAVs on their own. The electric automobile industry has benefitted from government incentives available to both manufacturers and buyers that have helped the electric automobile mature and integrate into day-to-day life. If the PAV is to ever exist, government or private subsidies will need to exist, at least initially, to make manufacturing and purchasing a PAV an attractive financial decision.

In 2005, NASA announced the NASA Centennial Challenge as part of NASA's Innovative Partnership Program for encouraging advances in personal aircraft efficiency and adaptability to PAV-like roles. In conjunction with the CAFE Foundation, two PAV challenges were held, one in 2007 and the other in 2008. While not directly working with industry to develop new technologies for use in future PAVs, these challenges gave a small monetary incentive for individuals interested in the future of the PAV to try and develop PAV-like features for their own, private, general aviation aircraft.

More recently, NASA has invested in development of a new X-Plane, most recently dubbed the X-57. While the X-57 does not exactly fit the PAV definition, many aspects and technologies that NASA is experimenting with for use on the X-57 have direct compatibility to use in future PAVs. In addition to the new technology being developed for use on the X-57, NASA is using a different approach for developing the X-57. NASA is partnering with small industry companies that are able to design and fabricate components for the X-57 aircraft faster than NASA can, as reported in the November 2016 edition of EAA's Sport Aviation magazine: [3]

> *Mark Moore, "X-57" principal investigator at NASA Langley, and Sean Clark, co-principal investigator at NASA Armstrong, are leading teams partnered with small businesses. "NASA has incredible depth and thousands of researchers who are the best in*

the world," Mark said. "However, we're the government and relatively slow moving. By merging with industry we are able to get the best of both worlds. These small companies are rapid in executing their portions of work. This project is moving incredibly fast." Empirical Systems Aerospace, the primary contractor, has a long history of contracts with NASA. Joby Aviation is designing and building new electric motors and motor controllers. Electric Power Systems is designing the lithium-ion battery system. Xperimental is building the new DEP (Distributed Electric Propulsion) carbon composite wing (As an interesting note, since this article was published, the development and production of the DEP carbon composite wing has been moved to Catto Propellers. This is a good example of just how fast things can change in the aerospace industry). The project uses MT propellers as well as NASA-designed propellers. Scaled Composites is installing the battery system and integrating the new electric motors onto the...aircraft.

A few lines farther down the article:

To encourage and incentivize U.S. industry to be a leader and not a distant follower, NASA and the FAA have teamed with industry to conduct emerging technology workshops. "We're not moving at the snail's pace that aerospace has been working at for the past 30 years. It's happening fast and furious. We want to help shepherd this technology to move as quickly as possible," Mark said.

It is really neat that NASA is utilizing small companies in the aerospace industry to develop an X-Plane that will result in advances in technology usable in future PAVs. As mentioned in the article, this is proving to be a very efficient way to develop an aircraft and help boost an industry. This is just what the aerospace industry needs to accelerate the maturity of the PAV. The increased rate in advances in aerospace, as mentioned in the last part of the article, is promising. Whether or not it is promising enough to bring us the PAV in the next fifty years is yet to be determined.

Overall

Overall, the PAV is an intriguing and viable idea that will make personal transportation faster, safer, and more convenient. Unfortunately the many factors needed to create an air vehicle that fits the definition of the PAV have just not come together to the point where the PAV is yet possible. To sum up a few of the major factors:

1. PAVs will need to use state of the art (expensive) materials to attain the desired speed and endurance.
2. PAVs will need to use a propulsion system with capabilities currently not in existence.
3. PAVs will need <u>many</u> small airports (that don't yet exist) to be operationally practical.
4. PAVs will need to be financially attainable, yet modern general aviation aircraft are not.
5. PAVs will need to change (and will need a change in) the public's perception of flying in a small personal aircraft.

Yes, current aerodynamics, structures, materials, computer automation, and some current infrastructure are all matured for use in a PAV, but there is just no suitable power plant for the PAV. This is where the PAV as a technology is stuck then. It is stuck waiting for another technology to mature, a technology that may take a very long time. Based on the current level of maturity of the other technologies required for use in the PAV, and how those technologies will continue to improve and mature in the future, there is no doubt that once a suitable power plant emerges the PAV will mature very rapidly, quickly overcoming sociological and other small technological hurdles.

So, will my grandchildren fly to my house to visit, or fly to a friend's house for a play date, or fly to the grocery store for food? Will my grandchildren watch constant streams of PAVs flying above them every day? Based on the current rate of technological maturity and social acceptance, it seems unlikely. However technological maturity is impossible to predict, and new discoveries could lead the PAV down the road to rapid success soon. I am confident however, that the PAV will mature eventually. The PAV will continue to be that elusive and attractive challenge occupying the minds of the world's greatest aircraft designers until finally the challenge can be solved. It will take time, but undoubtedly, it will happen.

1. "CAFE Foundation & The GAT Challenge." CAFE Foundation & The GAT Challenge. Accessed November 14, 2016. http://cafe.foundation/v2/pav_archive.php.
2. Seeley, Brien A. "Why Personal Air Vehicles?" Accessed November 14, 2016. http://cafe.foundation/v2/pav_general_why.php.
3. "Four Forces on an Airplane." NASA. Accessed December 12, 2016. https://www.grc.nasa.gov/www/k-12/airplane/forces.html.
4. Coates, Michael. "Pipistrel Sinus, Virus, Taurus, Apis LSA Aircraft Motorgliders for USA Gliders." Pipistrel Sinus, Virus, Taurus, Apis LSA Aircraft Motorgliders for USA Gliders. September 2007. Accessed December 12, 2016. http://www.pipistrel-usa.com/newsletters/newsletter-40/newsletter-40.html.
5. Stanton, Beth E. "The Sceptor X-57 Demonstrator." Sport Aviation, November 2016, 14-15.
6. "NASA Electric Research Plane Gets X Number, New Name." NASA. June 17, 2016. Accessed December 12, 2016. https://www.nasa.gov/press-release/nasa-electric-research-plane-gets-x-number-new-name.

CHAPTER 8:

WHAT WILL YOUR GRANDCHILDREN SEE?

THE PREDICTIONS

Edited by: David G. Ullman, Emeritus Professor, Mechanical Engineering

The results from the previous chapters can be summarized as ten predictions. Each is based on consensus of the authors. Do note that these conclusions are United States centric in that they do take into account international borders nor the economies and drivers of other nations.

While much effort has been made to produce the best predictions, they are weak in the consideration of government regulations, societal changes, air traffic control challenges and infrastructure needs. Each of these is briefly discussed before the predictions are made.

Government Regulations

Government regulation can greatly affect the outcome of the predictions. Currently, the Federal Aviation Administration (FAA) is working to establish rules for electric airplanes. But technology is often moving faster than the rules can evolve.

For example, electric airplanes have batteries that do not change in weight during flight as does expendable aviation fuel. Existing FAA rules for an ultralight aircraft, for example, requires an empty weight of 254 lbs (115 kg). The weight of the fuel is not counted in this requirement. Thus, any batteries carried reduce the allowable structural weight. The FAA has refused to count the equivalent fuel weight and raise the 254 lbs to allow for the batteries. This has resulted in very few commercial builders of ultralight aircraft bothering with electric propulsion.

A second example is that electric airplanes may have many small electric motors rather than a few internal combustion engines. A multi-engine pilot license is required for any aircraft having two or more engines. Thus a general aviation pilot rated for a single engined aircraft may not be sufficiently licensed to fly a multi engined electric aircraft. Additionally, it is not clear how the FAA will license a pilot for an airplane with say 20 small electric motors. Thus, as with aircraft weight, the government rules may hinder the development of new and unique forms of air travel.

Societal Changes

It is clear that society's attitude toward flight has greatly evolved over the first hundred years, progressing from the early daredevils to safe, widespread commercial travel. Yet many are still reluctant to fly at all and many more won't fly in a general aviation airplane. This "fear-of-flying" may change with the advent of autonomous flight, but it is hard to know if the "fear" will increase or decrease. As pointed out in Chapter 7 fear-of-flying is one of the reasons that Personal Air Vehicles (PAVs) may not find widespread acceptance.

As of this writing it is not clear how well the public will accept autonomous automobiles, so any conjecture on acceptance of autonomous aircraft is very problematic.

Air Traffic Control Challenges

The predictions forecast for more aircraft, yet we have not addressed how this traffic will be controlled. Current Air Traffic Control (ATC) does a good job of managing commercial and civil traffic. However, it is clear that there will be many more drones in the airspace (see Prediction 4) and other types aircraft may become more common. The rules for the use of drones are just evolving during the writing of this book and there has yet to be a drone-aircraft accident. Further, the use of autonomous aircraft (Prediction 5) will need to be integrated into the ATC system.

Infrastructure Needs

Changes in the types of aircraft and the frequency of flights will require changes in infrastructure. Proposals for some PAV systems call for pocket airports, small airports that support STOL or VTOL aircraft spaced conveniently around population centers. While this does not appear realistic (see Prediction 6) the other predictions, if they hold true will require infrastructure enhancements to support them.

The Predictions

With these limitations in mind, our predictions are:

Prediction 1: Our grandchildren will see bluer skies.

In spite of a predicted increase in air traffic, airplanes will be cleaner leading to less emissions and cleaner skies. While there will be many drones (see Prediction 4), most drones will be electric with the electricity coming from clean sources. Drones requiring longer flight times may be hybrid, but the motive sources will be small and designed for efficiency. Commercial transportation will continue to grow, but at the same time get cleaner and more efficient.

General aviation will be a mix of internal combustion engines, hybrids and electrics. Some of the airplanes flying now will still be in the air and using tried-and-true, air-cooled, gas fueled, internal combustion engines. Diesel powered airplanes will become more common. But new additions to the fleet will include hybrid powered airplanes and all electric airplanes.

Prediction 2: Our grandchildren will see flying wings carrying passengers and cargo.

While commercial airplanes have maintained their cigar shape for over fifty years, a new generation of airliners and cargo carriers will emerge. With both Boeing and Airbus, the two largest commercial aircraft producers in the world, pushing to make flight more efficient they are both experimenting with flying wing configurations. Rather than calling them "flying wings", a term associated with Northrop, they are referring to them as Blended-Wing-Bodies (BWBs). The B2 bomber introduced over 20 years was a harbinger of the BWBs to come.

The driver behind the BWB configuration is efficiency. By blending the wings and the fuselage, and removing the tail surfaces, the drag is lowered. Further efficiency is gained by making these aircraft larger, resulting in substantial interior spaces and increased wing spans.

While this type of configuration is ideal for cargo transport, there are two major downsides for commercial passenger flight. First, the large size creates problems with existing airport taxiways and terminals. Secondly, since many more passengers can be packed into an airplane with theater type seating, there is a passenger safety issue. Namely, in order for manufacturers to pass the full-scale demonstrations for new aircraft, all passengers and crew must evacuate the aircraft and be on the ground in 90 seconds or less. With the cigar style aircraft and its narrow rows of passengers this is challenging, for the theater seating of a BWB, this may be impossible.

Prediction 3: Our Grandchildren will see supersonic airliners

While the Concorde has come and gone, the desire for economical supersonic flight has not dimmed. It currently takes seven to eight hours to fly from NY to Paris; the Concorde did it in three and half hours. Companies like Airbus promise even faster speed with their next generation supersonic aircraft.

With increasing demand in air travel and the value of people's time, there is certainly market drivers pushing for this capability. It is anticipated that the next supersonic passenger carrying aircraft will not be airliners at all but business jets. These smaller aircraft are aimed at executives and heads of state, people who will find value with increased speed. Further, technical problems such as high noise and fuel consumption can more easily be addressed with these smaller aircraft.

Prediction 4: Our grandchildren will see drones, lots of drones.

The use of drones is currently evolving at a rapid rate. Exactly which markets will drive their adoption and their final form is still very uncertain. As discussed in Chapter 6, drones may evolve to fill needs in many different industries such as power line inspection, crop monitoring, medical response, package delivery or others, yet to be identified. Whatever drives their adoption, it is clear the will be lots of them in the sky. Some will take the form of quadcopters, some VTOL aircraft and others will be more conventional airplane-type configurations.

This adoption will come with many challenges. A primary one will be air-space management - what will keep them from running into each other, fixed objects and other non-drone aircraft? The answer may be captured in their autonomy, addressed in the next prediction.

However, it is unclear what laws will evolve that not only manage the air space, but define landing zones and protect people's privacy. Defining exactly where drones can land is more than a purely technical issue as it has marked societal and safety implications. These conflate with privacy issues. Just where drones can look, land and sense may greatly affect society.

Prediction 5: Our grandchildren will see autonomous airplanes.

The only airplanes that currently fly autonomously are military. However, as this book is being written, autonomous cars are being adopted and it is generally accepted that autonomous flight is simpler than autonomous road travel. Thus, it is clear that autonomous flight will develop. This will happen first with drones, then possibly happen commercially, and may happen with general aviation.

Drones will fly autonomously for power line inspection, crop monitoring, medical response, package delivery and other uses. They will be able to take off, navigate safely to their destination, perform any enroute mission, and land in an appropriate location, all automatically. Their adoption is dependent on not only technology evolution, but on laws and societal acceptance as discussed in Prediction 4.

Commercial aircraft in 2016 can already take off, navigate, and land without human aid. However, there is the need for pilots in the cockpit for emergencies, much decision making, and abnormalities. However, there is a reluctance of the general public to feel safe when control is out of their hands. Much will be learned about how people adopt to autonomy over the next couple of years during the early adoption of autonomous cars. This knowledge will help drive the evolution of autonomous airplanes.

With a current and increasing shortage of pilots there is an incentive to automate what we can. An initial area that may mature for our grandchildren to see is autonomous flights delivering cargo and mail. Here there is low risk to human life and there can be ground-based back-up pilots to take over in case of emergencies.

Finally, general aviation is a very small market made up mostly of hobbyists. Due to its small size and the hands-on nature of general aviation there is little incentive for the development of autonomous flight in this area. Any autonomy here is a move toward Person Air Vehicles, discussed in Prediction 6.

Prediction 6: Our grandchildren will <u>not</u> see Personal Air Vehicles.

While NASA and the Cafe Foundation push for the development of Personal Air Vehicles (PAVs) or air taxis that can take non-pilot passengers virtually door-to-door, the development of this capability is seen as dim.

As discussed in Chapter 7, there are many reasons for this prediction:
6. PAVs are predicated on the use of many small airports near to destinations, dotted around population centers. At a time when the number of airports is dwindling, it is hard to see how pocket airports (the Cafe concept) or landing zones in throughway clover leaf green areas (the NASA vision) will find public acceptance.
7. PAVs rely on autonomous flight. As addressed in Prediction 5, this may come about for cargo carrying and other non-human carrying flight vehicles, but is unlikely for human transportation.
8. PAVs would need to be inexpensive to be widely adopted. Whether they are marketed as a commercial fleet such as a taxi, or privately owned, they will need to be affordable. Based on the current cost of a general aviation airplane at well over $150,000 apiece, this seems unlikely.
9. The desire for a 150 -200 mph air-car is technically difficult on two fronts. First, most current general aviation aircraft cannot achieve these speeds and no technology is in development that will give them that capability economically (and non-polluting) and

inexpensively. Further, the concept of an air-car has been a dream for nearly one hundred years yet most current general aviation aircraft are cramped, uncomfortable, noisy and very un-car like.

Prediction 7: Our grandchildren will see more of what we have now.

Aviation changes very slowly. Designs in the commercial fleet have a lifetime of over 25 years. The Boeing 737 made its maiden flight in 1967 and variants of it are still being produced today with more planned[i]. In spite of all the improvements and modifications over the years, all 737s look similar. The same is true for other commercial models with the common cigar shaped fuselage and swept wings, a common sight today and will be so for the foreseeable future.

Further, most general aviation aircraft look the same as they have for years. In fact, in 2008, the average age of the general aviation fleet was nearly 50 years[ii]. While many newer general aviation aircraft are made of composites, little will change visually to those looking up.

This slow-to-change characteristic has been pointed out repeatedly in earlier chapters and has tempered all the predictions made. The exception will be the addition of drones as discussed in Prediction 4.

Prediction 8: Our grandchildren will see new materials

The evolution of new materials and manufacturing methods will not be obvious to the observers of flight, but will have an impact on the types, configurations and performance of aircraft. To a high degree, virtually all the other predictions will be affected by the success in the development, production and use of new materials.

More airplanes will be built that are more than 50% composite by weight like the Boeing 787 and Airbus A350. This trend will be fueled by improved and less costly composite manufacturing methods. Additionally, newer composites will be in use with ceramic matrices and carbon fibers increasing the physical properties that enable weight reduction.

While the use of composites will grow, the metals industry will be busy developing super alloys to compete with them especially in engine components and with other high strength needs.

Prediction 9: Our grandchildren will see electric and hybrid aircraft.

In 2016, electric airplanes are in their infancy. While the promise is great, it is dependent on the maturation of battery energy density or the development of efficient hybrid systems. While the aviation market is not sufficiently large enough to drive the needed developments, the automobile market is. Thus, the advancements that will enable the maturation of electric and hybrid ground vehicles will also enable the development of similarly powered aircraft. Should the ground vehicle development falter, so too will the odds of this prediction being realized.

While the large airplane manufacturers are seriously studying hybrid airliners, it is anticipated that acceptance will come first in general aviation. The main drivers will be economy of flight and a desire to reduce pollution and noise. Expect to see both manufacturers and hobbyists explore new configurations that optimize the use of electric propulsion.

Prediction 10: Our grandchildren will see more airplanes in the sky.

With the maturation of drones and the continuing increase in commercial air traffic, the skies will become more crowded. This will lead to the need for improved air traffic control, cleaner propulsion and new laws and regulations.

In summary, the future of atmospheric aviation looks bright. The next thirty five years will see more-of-the-same mixed with radically new aircraft. The continued demand for air travel, balanced by the demand for cleaner, faster and quieter passenger travel, combined with the advent of the drones will certainly change the view our grandchildren will see.

[ii] 2013 General Aviation Statistical Databook and 2014 Industry Outlook, General Aircraft Manufacturers Association (GAMA), 2013, page 34, https://www.gama.aero/files/GAMA%202013%20Databook-Updated-LowRes.pdf

Made in the USA
San Bernardino, CA
08 March 2017